Religion and Humane Global Governance

Religion and Humane Global Governance

Richard Falk

palgrave

RELIGION AND HUMANE GLOBAL GOVERNANCE
Copyright © Richard Falk, 2001.
All rights reserved. No part of this book may be used or reproduced in any manner whatsoever without written permission except in the case of brief quotations embodied in critical articles or reviews.

First published 2001 by
PALGRAVE™
175 Fifth Avenue, New York, NY 10010 and
Houndmills, Basingstoke, Hampshire, England RG21 6XS.
Companies and representatives throughout the world.

Palgrave is the new global publishing imprint of St Martin's Press LLC Scholarly and Reference Division and Palgrave Publishers Ltd (formerly Macmillan Press Ltd).

ISBN 0-312-23337-X hardback
Library of Congress Cataloging-in-Publication Data

Falk, Richard A.
  Religion and humane global governance / Richard Falk.
    p. cm.
  Includes index.
  ISBN 0-312-23337-X
  1. Religion and international affairs. 2. Globalization—Religious aspects. I. Title.

BL65.I55 .F35 2001
291.1'787—dc21
                            00-068845

Design by Newgen Imaging Systems (P) Ltd.

First Edition: June 2001
10 9 8 7 6 5 4 3 2 1

Printed in the United States of America.

For Kekuni Blaisdell
James Douglass
Chandra Muzaffar

tireless sojourners
of diverse faith,
visionaries,
exemplary citizen pilgrims

Contents

Acknowledgments	ix
Introduction	1
1. The Religious Foundations of Humane Global Governance	13
2. Secularism in an Era of Globalization	35
3. The Monotheistic Religions and Globalization	61
4. Religion and Politics: Verging on the Postmodern	77
5. Politically Engaged Spirituality in an Emerging Global Civil Society	101
6. Hans Küng's Crusade: Framing a Global Ethic	123
7. Gandhi's Legacy for World Order	143
8. Our Millennial Challenge	157
Notes	167
Index	187

Acknowledgments

This book, more than most, benefits from friendships, direct experience, and a process of non-academic reflection. I have been deeply influenced over the years by varying degrees of encounter with a range of faith traditions. In important respects this process started when I was an undergraduate at the University of Pennsylvania and had the benefit of several demanding courses with an inspired and brilliant teacher of religious thought, Edwin E. Aubrey. Later, while at Yale Law School, I made a rather intensive study of Indian law and religion, having the benefit of work with Professor F. S. C. Northrop, whose book *The Meeting of East and West* left an enduring imprint on my imagination. During these years I went so far in this direction as to spend more time trying to learn Sanskrit than on any of my law subjects.

Later, while a graduate law student at Harvard in the late 1950s, I attended three courses of Paul Tillich, and had the opportunity to read Martin Buber, Karl Jaspers, and Søren Kierkegaard. As a result, my approach to politics and law never altogether felt comfortable with either the ethics or epistemology of scientific humanism, and even less so with the prevailing orthodoxy of political realism. This volume seeks to express a receptivity to religious and spiritual perspectives without turning a blind eye toward extremist forms of belief that have done so much to give religion a bad name in both secular circles, and even more so, among those who are at once devout and inclusive.

I wish, especially, to acknowledge the three individuals to whom I have dedicated my book: Kekuni Blaisdell, James Douglass, and Chandra Muzaffar. I have been privileged to work with each of these exceptional human beings, and to bear witness to the depth of their religious and spiritual commitments, as well as to their persevering struggle for justice and peace often in the face of daunting obstacles. Each has been an exemplary leader, rooted in faith and belief, and holding firm against entrenched structures of abuse, militarism, and distortion.

There are others who have also encouraged me in a similar direction at various times, and happily, often in the course of friendship, and even intimacy. I would mention Renée Weber, Sally Appleton, William Sloan Coffin, Catherine Keller, Lester Ruiz, David Ray Griffin, Charlene Spretnak, Charles Jencks, Daniel Berrigan, Philip Berrigan, Liz McAlister, Tu Weiming, William Irwin Thompson, Richard Baker, Barbara Baudot and Ahmet Davutoglu as important presences at various stages of my life. I have also been privileged to be part of three networks of exceptional individuals seeking to find ways to bring knowledge, spirituality, and citizenship into a single fused understanding: The Lindisfarne Association, The Portrack Seminars, and The Triglav Circle.

I was also deeply affected by a visit to Iran in 1979 during the final phase of the Islamic Revolution. During that visit I had the opportunity to have extended discussions with a range of religious leaders, including Ayatollah Ruhollah Khomeini, and to gain some understanding of both the extraordinary mobilizing and emancipatory power of a resurgent Islam and of its dangerous tendency to adopt a totalizing approach that is essentially intolerant and oppressive. I later understood that this double-edged potency is characteristic of all the major world religions, which suggests the importance of combining a posture of receptivity with that of critical concern.

I would also like to make some more customary acknowledgments. As so often in the past, the Center of International Studies, and it recent director, Michael Doyle, have been supportive of my work and helped to provide the academic auspices that made it possible. As so many times over the years, I have been helped in numerous ways in the preparation of this manuscript for publication by my excellent secretary and assistant, June Garson. And at a crucial stage, I was the beneficiary of the efficient and gracious secretarial assistance of Marcia Lynch.

I also want to acknowledge the help, efficiency, and warmth of my contact with Palgrave. I was especially fortunate to have had such excellent copyediting help from Jen Simmington, and at the last stages from Sabahat Chaudhary. It was Karen Wolny who encouraged me initially to proceed with this venture, and Gabriella Pearce who was accommodating and helpful throughout the journey. I am grateful to them all.

My wife, Hilal, has shared with me, in every respect, the long process of turning vague gropings into a finished book. Her love and vitality provide a continuing source of inspiration and delight.

Finally, let me acknowledge, with gratitude, those who have given their permission for me to draw on previously published work in *Global Dialogue* (Centre for World Dialogue), *ReVision* (Heldref Publications), *International Journal of Politics, Culture and Society* (Kluwer Academic/Plenum Publishers), and *Humanity*. I would also like to thank Peter Lang Publishing, Inc., State University of New York Press, and B. R. Publishing Corp. (Delhi, India) for giving permission to rely on material previously published as chapters in edited books appearing under their imprint.

Introduction

Gaining Perspective on the Present

Nothing has shocked, angered, and confused the modern, secular sensibility more than the return of religion to the mainstream of political life in an array of settings around the world. Mocking both our capacity to overcome our past and anticipate our future, this religious resurgence converges with an era of unprecedented and radical technological innovation that is also subverting the sensibility and lifeworld of modernity in ways that we are only beginning to realize. Such a start for the new millennium presents both extraordinary opportunities for enhancing the material and spiritual life of peoples inhabiting the planet and severe dangers to the wellbeing, and even the survival, of the human species. Among the ironies of the present is this strange mixture of technological dynamism that exceeds the most grandiose promises of the Enlightenment and a new wave of skepticism directed toward the role of science and reason in shaping our sense of reality.

The religious resurgence comes in many forms, not all welcome but certainly not all an occasion of regret, much less menace. To the extent that the new wave of religion is animated mainly by negative spiritual energy, that is, by unconditional and extreme moves to negate the modern, it tends to be destructive of human potentiality, to deny freedom, to claim an exclusive access to truth, to be regressively-other worldly in its promises of salvation, and to fail to provide humanity with positive ways forward. It revives a widespread sense among moderate sensibilities that organized religion is an obstacle to be overcome. But there are other more positive and emancipatory energies also contained in this renewal of religion that are associated with a reaffirmation of the spiritual sense of the person, a feeling for the sacred and the mystery that lies at the heart of human existence, an embrace of human solidarity, and a recognition that spiritual longing and religious tradition can take many authentic forms that offer us many evocative metaphors for truth and ultimate concern that no human agency can grasp with infallibility.

Undoubtedly, part of this recent lure of religion is as an antidote to the homogenizing impacts of the false universalism and runaway consumerism associated with a new post-Marxist economism that represents the latest phase of capitalism and is an ambitious project of the West to establish the first world megacivilization under its dominion. The United States occupies a special role in this unfolding global drama, being the main source of the most innovative market practices, the most active purveyor of a new economistic global ideology, and the toughest and most adept guarantor of "law and order" by virtue of its planetary military prowess and its interventionary diplomacy. It is in America that this battlefield among creativity, species suicide, and religious awakening is likely to be fought out in the decades ahead, for it is on its frontiers that the revolutionary transformations of biotechnology, genetic engineering, robotics, and molecular electronics are likely first to present profound and dramatic questions about identity and existence. Of course such a struggle over identities and fundamental issues will resonate throughout the world and cannot be confined, or even centered, within a particular territorial domain, however powerful.

Who are we? Can we control the machines that we have developed? Do we even want to have at our disposal such awesome power to extend life, to design human beings, to download software and hardware in such a way to fulfill dreams (and nightmares) of omnipotence and immortality? Should we impose limits on inquiry and application, thereby challenging the most basic affirmation of the Enlightenment heritage, the freedom to inquire and to know? How shall we strike a new balance between freedom and regulation? What boundaries shall identify the authority structures of the future? And what institutions shall administer laws and dispense justice? The primitive form of these questions is currently raised in relation to such matters as intellectual property rights on the Internet and off-shore money laundering and tax havens. The state is groping for new modes of regulatory effectiveness in this era of diminished territoriality, at least for money and elites. But these issues are but foretastes of what lies ahead, a time when human cloning will pose a choice between upholding the autonomy of human evolution as we have previously understood it and a societally managed evolutionary process that will almost inevitably make eugenics the queen of the sciences. We face choices also about the outer limits of artificial intelligence, the brilliant robot that can be sent on lethal missions, or worse, robot armies and air forces that can be programmed to devastate a less-developed adversary without risk or casualty. Do we not need desperately a spiritual ground from which to pose such questions before they are foreclosed by technological momentum, decisions behind closed doors, and economic/political ambition?

On one level the relation of religion to these emergent economic, political, and cultural forces is a reflexive flourish that expresses hysteria and little else. A Greek Orthodox cleric, Archbishop Christodoulos *cri de coeur* is typical: "Resist, my dear Christians, the forces of globalization and religious marginalization are out to get you."[1] The struggle, so conceived, is mindlessly against modernity itself rather than against its menacing extremities and an accompanying false universalism that is globe-encircling. Those who demonstrated in the streets of Seattle against the inequities of globalization, which they attributed to the World Trade Organization (WTO) (and its sibling institutions, the World Bank and the International Monetary Fund [IMF]), and who vandalized a McDonald's in France shared the simplistic view that it is possible and desirable to hold back the march of history by postures of defiance. It is the contention of this book that neither the disease nor the cure are so obvious, that we must look deeply into our individual and collective past, and that we need to fashion visions of a preferred future that can mobilize the positive energies of humanity in whatever religious, cultural, or political form they assume. Because the globalizing reality is undeniable, the moment for a critical ethical ecumenism has arrived. The critical element ensures that only those ethical orientations that are consistent with the broad premises of a human rights culture are affirmed. Precisely because this ecumenical moment has arrived, there is widespread fear, foreboding, and a disposition to retreat into the closed and rigid structures of the past, both a traditionalist past and a blinkered secularism that represents a degeneration of the modern impulse toward freedom, reason, and autonomy.

The complexity of the challenge arises because it is not usefully reducible to either the dualisms of good and evil or the assured remedies of this or that fundamentalism. It is neither possible to affirm unconditionally the main tendencies of modernity, including ideas about sovereignty, the territorial state, and the right of self-determination on the political sensibility, nor useful to pretend that such defining categories have been superseded by such fashionable phrases as "the end of the nation-state," "the borderless world," "a new medievalism," or "the end of history." More suitable for the age are such ideas as that of "negative capability," associated with the musing of the English poet John Keats, who thought of a mature mind as one that did not press for answers prematurely. Being able to accept uncertainty as the outer limit of knowability is an emphasis that has been featured in the postmodernist insistence that most of human life consists of choices that are by their nature "undecidable." Also helpful are Eastern patterns of thought, perhaps most fully and clearly embodied in the Hindu worldview, which affirms that opposites coexist in experienced reality and cannot be eliminated without generating crippling distortions. Such notions are not easily accepted in the West, which has premised its development on a classical Greek heritage that was itself built upon an either/or foundation for knowledge, thought, action, and belief. There are two elements here that are easily confounded. The first is that the human mind, capable of so much that is ingenious, is also at a loss when it comes to grasping the fullness of reality. The second is that the rationalistic device of dividing choices into dualisms creates an illusion about the comprehension of alternatives but is reductive and essentialist in actuality, pretending that reality can be adequately understood to be either "this" or "that."

Introducing Humane Global Governance

The idea of humane global governance is in the process of formation and partakes of many kindred impulses, including those associated with human rights, democracy, justice, and spirituality. Encouragement of multicultural conversation and collaboration is found in imagining a future that is beneficial for humanity as a whole and working toward its achievement. Perhaps, most of all, such an imagined future expresses the mood of some lines from Orhan Pamuk's novel *The Black Book*: "We live but for a short time, we see but very little, and we know almost nothing; so, at least, let's do some dreaming."[2]

Putting the word "humane" before "global governance" is a deliberate situating of value-oriented concerns at the center of inquiry. It is linked to both the more functionalist and pragmatic claims associated with proposals for "global governance" and to a series of ethical affirmations and aspirations.[3] On a practical level it acknowledges the needs for more effective global institutions, but it shifts the focus from management to human wellbeing, and it puts less hope in the wisdom and compassion of the existing world leadership than on the oppositional forces aligned with a mélange of transnational social forces and an emergent global civil society. And it is there that civilizational and religious renewal can help by nourishing and mobilizing a vision of the possible and necessary that is anchored in human solidarity as well as in distinct traditions of morality, compassion, and spirituality.[4]

Any adequate approach to humane global governance must be grounded in the realities of material unevenness that exist within societies and regions and among the states that compose world order. This unevenness is also embodied in the anguish of extreme poverty and the decadence of superwealth. Even the demeaning absurdity of the U.N. measure of poverty, defined as earning less than $1 per day, results in the astounding number of 1.2 billion poor. The global managers and their stastically minded spin doctors have led us to regard the world as much less agonized than is the case. If more realistic measures were adopted, well over half of the world's population would be understood as living under conditions of acute economic deprivation, an intolerable circumstance and one that is potentially explosive. At the other end of the socioeconomic spectrum are a tiny privileged elite with control over billions of dollars, with more resources than most governments, and with a capacity to use such resources in wasteful, manipulative, or beneficial ways. This consumptive pattern often includes luxuries and leisure that the pampered psyches of these elites cannot handle. Such wealth and economic rewards combined with the hardship endured by those who toil to survive manifests an unjust set of connections between work and reward that must be concealed to discourage discontent and a reemergence of the class struggle that disturbed the peace in the early stages of national capitalism. The injustice is greater than what results from the failure to address poverty and avoidable human suffering as a priority concern. It exceeds also the mere fact of gross inequality of capacity and circumstances. A humane political order would not necessarily succeed in eliminating economic privation or seek to do away altogether with inequality, but it would dedicate itself to the fulfillment of the basic human needs of all people, it would put some upper limits on economic rewards and the accumulation and inheritance of wealth, and, above all, it would support a global ethos based on empathy, compassion, and nonviolence.

The prospects for humane global governance do not seem bright at the present. Global civil society is weak and divided, and it has not coalesced around a common vision of the future. The collaboration between leading governments and global market forces is, by contrast, strong and durable, highlighted by the power of business and finance to put limits on the democratic electoral process throughout the world and by the discipline of global capital that is able to inhibit most moves toward greater equity in the distribution of economic rewards. Such a reconfiguring of power has produced "a new geopolitics" that adapts the state and its governing elites to the realities of a capital-driven world order.

Confronting the Westphalian Legacy

As previously noted, the Information Age, with its disavowal of boundaries and limits, imperils the state as an effective problem-solver for a growing range of nonterritorial activities. But it would be a glaring mistake of an economistic or cybernetic mindset to overlook the persisting potency of the state with regard to most matters of human wellbeing, including the movement of ordinary people (not elites) and the control of their lives. The Westphalian state remains both a sanctuary (for refugees) and a maximum security prison (for captive minorities and nationalities). For a people trapped within an alien state, the idea of secession is a necessary dream, often the only viable escape route from vulnerability and oppression, and acknowledged, although in a controversial form, through the affirmation of the right of self-determination inhering in all peoples.[5] Yet there is another side of this equation that cannot be ignored: Open borders in a world of severe unevenness pose a threat to a historic community's sense of special character. Should not a territorially bounded community have the option of protecting its cultural identity against an onslaught from without that, if unrestricted, would engulf the more successful societies of the world with hordes of desperate and unwanted migrants? Such "invasions" also risk a variety of racist, rightist, backlash responses that imperil democratic forms of governance, human rights, and societal moderation. Similarly, "exclusions" of those who are desperate invites criminality, including various smuggling operations that deposit these hapless persons in distant lands at great profit. As matters now stand, there are uneasy compromises being struck around the world between advocates of identity politics and those who support the same freedom of movement for people as now pertains to the movement of money and information.

An insistence on the juridical linking of nationality to the state has made the sovereign state into a confusing, contradictory foundation for identity and allegiance. It can foster purification moves of great variety, in extreme cases with genocidal implications, when the state is mythically and exclusively connected with a particular nationality, the romantic conception of the nation-state that has bedeviled the German past and is causing such havoc of late in the south Balkans and elsewhere. But the state can also disseminate a pedagogy of tolerance and diversity, as when nationality is reduced to juridical power protective of the human rights of the entire political community. Such a government confers nationality through rituals of citizenship and fosters a multinational society that preaches and practices nondiscrimination. The U.S. mainstream is attempting to overcome its racist past by embracing these ideals, despite a distrust of a unified whole, which is expressed by minorities in the form of multiculturalism. The nation-state is thus a profoundly ambiguous political animal in relation to the project of humane global governance. It is at once the main obstacle to its attainment and the necessary agency for its pursuit.

This ambiguity also pertains to the assertion of international human rights as imperative duties for states, the violation of which raises questions of accountability for governments and their leaders. At what point should the wider international community intercede—by force if necessary—to rescue a society, or a part of society, from oppressive government? Should this matter be invariably decided by the U.N. Security Council, or must it be left to the ad hoc assessments made in each case? The doctrine of humanitarian intervention, so much debated in the aftermath of the NATO war over Kosovo in 1999, suggests that these issues are both salient and unresolved. It is intolerable for the world to watch the unfolding of genocidal dramas exemplifying the continuing supremacy of the sovereign state, but it is also questionable to entrust the mechanism of humanitarian intervention to the self-interested vagaries of geopolitics. Humane global governance would find the political space within which to respect the diversity and autonomy of states while still insisting on adherence to a rule of law that protects the elementary rights of individuals, groups, and peoples and has the means and mandate to act effectively in the event that gross abuses persist.

These matters of softening and balancing power have been generally entrusted to secular processes in modern states, but with varying results. It is time that the post-Enlightenment divide between religion and politics was drawn into question so that the great legal texts of human rights can receive a civilizational and societal ratification as well as a formal acceptance at the level of government. Such a process involves, first of all, a recognition that the claims and language of universality used to formulate human rights standards are but a thin veil thrown over a process that was dominated from the start by Western personalities, outlooks, and cultural standpoints and initiated in a global setting in which the main non-Western civilizations were either colonized or subordinated. It is here that the religious awakening can contribute to the formation of identities that link past and future, that bridge differences of civilizational belief, and above all, that can foster from positions of deep rootedness an understanding and celebration of a transcendent common humanity. The humanizing of the Westphalian framework is integral to the project of humane global governance.

It is neither possible nor feasible to dispense with the sovereign state as the central organizing reality for the collective social life of the planet. It is possible and necessary to make this state and its leaders accountable and to compensate for its loss of capacity to cope with many facets of globalization. Secularism, as emanating from the West, can be part of the dialogue of religions and civilizations pertaining to the future of the state, but it is not able on its own to gain legitimacy for its proposals on global governance. These proposals are both tainted by their Western format and influenced by economistic preoccupations, having so far led to much stronger market-oriented institutions for trade and investment than people-oriented institutions for human rights, peacekeeping, and development. Is it surprising that the IMF, WTO, and World Bank have almost effortlessly been recipients of major transfers of resources and entrusted with the capabilities to intrude on sovereignty at its core, whereas the United Nations is kept on the shortest possible financial leash and is viewed with suspicion and hemmed in with constraints at every turn?

The Way Forward: Exploration, Collaboration, and Reconciliation

The historical circumstances of religious revival, postcolonial rediscoveries of identity and claims for redress of past grievance, secularist self-doubts, and a variety of ideas and practices encompassed by the terminology of globalization are conditioning our understanding of world order and shaping alternative paths to the future. There are significant unifying circumstances arising from the global scope of telecommunications, solidarity in actions designed to reduce human suffering, a consensus about sustaining life prospects on the planet, and a willingness to affirm abstract adherence to human rights and democracy as the basis for legitimate governance.

Widespread efforts to reclaim non-Western civilizational identities involve an encouraging project to reach back in cultural history past the experiences of modernity and forward beyond the constraints of nationalism, statism, and a Western conception of progress and fulfillment. Such explorations are complemented by important experiments in regionalism, economic restructuring, and political and cultural relations on the basis of wider affinities that are rooted partly in pragmatic concerns about economic gains and security. These regional undertakings also incorporate shared ethical principles and values that provide the foundation for a political community that is wider than the statist demarcations of community under the Westphalian regime and yet narrower than the false universalism of schemes for unifying the world under a single source of authority or an exaggerated view of the impact of technology. Religions are part of this dynamic of regional self-exploration, creating transnational bonds and affinities that extend beyond state, nation, tribe, ethnic community, and language group.

In every respect, such developments partake of ambiguity and contradiction. The regional and the civilizational perspectives also create openings for exclusivist interpretations of the historical and human situation. It is plausible to construct a vision of the future based on the "West against the rest" that organizes a fragment of humanity to take part in intercivilizational warfare. It is also plausible to view the West as the "Great Satan" that must be destroyed as the precondition for self-realization throughout the planet.[6]

My idea in this book is to take a strand in favor of collaboration and reconciliation, but not with sentimental hopes that conflict will disappear or that humane institutions for global governance can be agreed upon in the years immediately ahead. Instead, the positive inclusive tendencies in secularism and religious outlooks need to bond, without subverting their distinctive forms of attentiveness to human suffering and aspiration, in the course of defining "humane globalization" for all peoples in the world. In this respect, the rigid separation of politics and religion that is under attack by conservatives in the West and is being supported by liberals needs to be reinterpreted at a time when various civilizations are both mingling in shared geographic space and searching for their own autonomy. Whether secularists like it or not, the questions just over the technological horizon are "religious" in character, reminding us of the dangers and temptations associated with going beyond prior limit conditions that have for centuries expressed the outer contours of human existence. These contours have included anthropocentrism in relation to natural surroundings and the products of human intelligence. What lies ahead are scenarios of blurred limitations and unavoidable soul-searching and, more mundanely, challenges about how to address current inequities, grievances, and survival risks. It is bound to be an exciting period that will shake the foundations of consumerism, the McWorld, and materialist worldviews, but it is also a menacing period that will generate idolatrous temptations to mechanize the fundaments of life itself, as well as give rise to death-oriented and salvationist cults that herald the end of the world.

At such times of turmoil, it is helpful to stand back and yet hold fast, affirming a commitment to work together while respecting the needs of the peoples of the world to consider separately what sort of future their specific heritages most favors at this point.[7] And yet not fall into new traps of civilizational and religiously grounded essentialism. Every collective identity is itself plural in its memories, perceptions, and potentialities and needs to address inner tensions as urgently as its relations with the domineering threat of renewed Western hegemony. And of course, the West, least of all, is exempt from this imperative to reconsider its identity under the pressure of criticism from without and from explosive prospects within, especially those associated with developments on the technological frontiers.

This book attempts no prescriptions, offers no recipes. It depicts a starting point that is responsive to dangers, potentialities, hopes, and dreams that are not normally incorporated into the study of world politics, or even emphasized in the more normative offerings of world order studies. It implicitly questions whether the premises of international relations can any longer be usefully comprehended by a reliance on realism, liberalism, Marxism, constructivism, and idealism, even taking account of their variability in and adaptability to a changing global setting. If its own orientation must be categorized, it comes closest to being a form of *reconstructive postmodernism*, that is, a post-Westphalian perspective that is informed by ethical values and spiritual belief.[8]

1.

The Religious Foundations of Humane Global Governance

Locating the Inquiry

The religious dimension of human experience has been generally excluded from the serious study and practice of governance for several centuries, especially in the West. The exclusion is definitely a consequence of the European Enlightenment and its endorsement of autonomous reason as the only reliable guide for human affairs, as well as its general tendency to ground politics upon a secular ethos, a principal feature of which is the separation of church and state. Of course, as with many questionable moves in history, this development had positive aspects and was rooted in a particular set of historical circumstances in Europe at the time of the formation of the modern state system, a process whose origin is difficult to locate with precision but is often, although somewhat arbitrarily, dated to coincide with the Peace of Westphalia in 1648.

Without entering into this complex story in any detail, the justification for the exclusion of religion had to do with the perception that religious institutions were inimical to the rise of science and material progress in human affairs and the undeniable reality that the split in Christendom had contributed to a series of terrible wars. The exclusion of religion always had certain normative costs, including the realization that religious attachments are so strong in society that religion, excluded from entering the front door of political life, will find other entrances, including concealed trap doors. The effects of this reassertion of religious relevance may be to obstruct an understanding of how public policies are actually being shaped.

So in an important sense, historically, it is necessary to understand that the exclusion of religion from political life was seen as a vital step in the ongoing struggle to establish humane governance, that is governance based on reason, religious and ethnic tolerance, gender equality, and the dignity of the individual human being. In many respects Hugo Grotius, a typical Renaissance figure, was generally regarded as the founder of modern international law and an intellectual figure who sensitively embodied the passing of Medieval Europe to the new Europe of independent, sovereign, territorial states. Grotius was a witness to the Thirty Years War that ravaged Europe and represented a struggle that was fought along the geographical and ideological fault line that separated Catholicism from Protestantism. Grotius was, in one sense, seeking to restore the religious possibility for human life by removing it from the violent rivalries of the political realm. In his vivid, often-quoted words, "Throughout the Christian world I observed a lack of restraint in relation to war, such as even barbarous races should be ashamed of; I observed that men rush to arms for slight causes, or no cause at all, and that when arms have once been taken up there is no longer any respect for law, divine or human; it is as if, in accordance with a general decree, frenzy had openly been let loose for the committing of all crimes."[1]

In adopting this critical stance Grotius combined two of the defining characteristics of modernity, a claim of moral superiority associated with the specific identity of "the Christian world" that should inform political life however possible and an implicit deprecation of non-Christian societies as the vast domain of "barbarous races." The first impulse led to the idea that the relations among states are to some extent governed by law, while the second gave a sort of underpinning to the Eurocentric conceptions of world order and hierarchical relations between Western and non-Western peoples that came to flourish in the colonial age. Such liberal rationalizations for the politics and structures of domination were later produced by the most admired Enlightenment figures: Hegel, Kant, and John Stuart Mill among others. Neither led to humane governance for the peoples of the world: International law was too weak to contain the passions of nationalism or dreams of empire, and the validation of colonial rule amounted to little more than a rationalization for the exploitation and domination of non-Western peoples and generated in many instances deep patterns of resentment that surfaced in the form of intense intrasocietal violence after independence.

There have been attempts in the recent past to associate this normative orientation toward political reality with an emergent and evolving world order that had within it the potentiality to achieve humane governance for the entire world. Hedley Bull, an influential Oxford professor of international law, depicted an international society of states that sustained a balance between sovereign rule within territorial limits and a kind of prudent moderation, safeguarded by the benevolence of leading military powers, in the relations among states, a type of world order described as an "anarchic society."[2] Myres McDougal, the founder of the New Haven School of Jurisprudence and International Law, together with a group of collaborators depicted the spread of Enlightenment values through the commitment to democratic types of public order systems as an evolving foundation for a humane intercivilizational pattern of governance that had the capacity to produce, eventually, a peaceful and equitable world order of benefit to the entire world.[3]

Both of these approaches to the future of world order were premised on the persistence of the states system as the basis of world order and in that sense were in some way rooted in anti-utopian traditions of political realism. Additionally, building on the heritage of Woodrow Wilson and the experiments in world organization represented by the League of Nations and the United Nations, there emerged a more utopian strain of secular thought that fundamentally believed that the only secure and legitimate form of world order depended upon the establishment of world government, a body of thought that came to be associated with world federalism and is probably still best represented by the work of Grenville Clark and Louis B. Sohn in the form of *World Peace through World Law*.[4]

Even the World Order Models Project (WOMP), with its explicit undertaking to consider the diverse world order perspectives representative of the leading regions and ideologies active in the world, failed to include in any serious or systematic manner the relevance of religion, although it did acknowledge that world order values, widely shared on an intercivilizational basis, provided the normative framing of any successful project to establish, or even to envisage, humane global governance.[5]

Although the perspectives arising from the work of Bull and McDougal remain useful as moderating guides with normative foundations for operations within the existing framework of world order, their regulative capabilities and potentialities seem far too modest to address the deficiencies of international political life that arise from the persistence of war and militarism, from the pervasiveness of poverty and economic deprivation, from the circumstances of political oppression and religious extremism, from the disregard of environmental decay and danger, and from the neglect of the spiritual sides of human nature and aspiration. The advocacy of world government as a normative project seems strangely discordant with the current weakening of support for even the feeble efforts to sustain existing world political organizations. Such weakening is epitomized by the recent travails of the United Nations, and although there is an increasingly frequent framing of political life in relation to the metaphor of a "global village," it is seen primarily as an expression of the potency of economic globalization or as expressive of the new borderless cyberworld of the internet.[6] In effect, the best of secular thinking falls short of providing either a plausible path to travel in pursuit of humane global governance or a sufficiently inspiring vision of its elements that would mobilize a popular grassroots movement for drastic global reform.[7]

This failure is partially due to the exclusion of religious and spiritual dimensions of human experience from the shaping of the vision and practices associated with the quest for global humane governance. This chapter intends an overview: first, a section on dominant world order trends and tendencies with respect to global governance; then some consideration of the extent to which these recent world order trends, which are shaping the historical situation at the start of the third millennium, are also creating new, unexpected openings for religious and spiritual energies, a development that also, as with the secularist era of exclusion, has deeply disturbing, as well as encouraging, aspects. This religious resurgence is discussed as part of the double-edged relevance of religion for the kind of global governance most likely to emerge. The final section argues for the inclusion of emancipatory religious and spiritual perspectives in world order thinking and practice, along with an enumeration of potential contributions.[8]

Current World Order Trends, or Pathways to Inhumane Governance

Without entering into a detailed inquiry, it seems evident that there are several dominant world order trends that are converging in such a way as to generate a more integrated form of governance at the global level, but in a form that undermines several critical world order values to a significant degree and thus qualifies the emergent new world order as a variant of "inhumane governance." Such an indictment is not meant to be a total condemnation. There are aspects of these globalizing developments that represent normative improvements on prior conditions (for instance, a reduction in the prospect for large-scale nuclear war, a diminishing likelihood of international warfare in general, and the alleviation of poverty and economic deprivation for hundreds of millions of people, particularly those living in several of the most populous, and previously some of the most severely and hopelessly impoverished, countries of the Pacific Rim), but the overall impact is to fracture the peoples of the world, to neglect the plight of those who are most deprived and vulnerable, to place nonsustainable burdens on the environment that seem likely to diminish the life quality of future generations, to deepen over time the disparities between rich and poor, and to engender an ethos of consumerism that forecloses the most fulfilling forms of individual and social self-realization.[9] As such, despite this mixed picture, it seems appropriate to describe the resultant arrangements of global governance as cumulatively contributing to "global inhumane governance."

The Dynamics of Economic Globalization

There is no doubt that the greater mobility of capital is facilitating a more materially efficient use of resources, if the benchmarks are the return on capital (profitability), economic growth, and the expansion of world trade. This pattern of global economic development is fostered, as well, by a global media that is one aspect of globalization, and is notable for its shameless promotion of a consumerist conception of human happiness and fulfillment in a societal setting of increasing inequality, persisting massive poverty, and growing anxiety. The interdependence of economic activity as well as the extraordinary complexity arising from spectacular technological innovations are creating a growing and manifest need for effective regional and global governance in the form of policy coordination and institutionalized regimes of control. The strength of global market forces is now such that existing governance structures at the level of the sovereign state are losing their political independence and autonomy; the discipline of global capital is becoming an iron cage constraining policy choice.[10] This pattern is most evident in relation to the heavily indebted countries of the

Global South, especially in the form of intrusions by the World Bank and IMF into the policymaking spheres of government. But the process is almost as evident in the affluent countries of the Global North that make seemingly spontaneous adjustments in their policy options to reflect the priorities of global capital and governing elites, encouraging fiscal austerity and subordinating societal claims on resources.[11]

The governance consequences are two-fold: (1) the creation of formal and informal arenas for the coordination of global economic policy according to the priorities of capital, and (2) the creation of institutional arrangements that can give behavioral effect to such priorities. In the first category one can mention the Annual Economic Summit of Industrial Countries, the so-called G-7, in which the heads of state of these leading countries gather each year in one of their member countries for several days of discussion and photo opportunity. These G-7 meetings are far less significant in relation to their substantive achievements than in signaling to the world the ascendancy of economistic forces within the global setting. The attention given to these economic summits far outweighs the participation of these leaders in the activities of the United Nations where it is rare indeed for any leader to remain in attendance for more than a few hours, if at all. An informal arena along the same lines, although operating in a more obscure fashion, is the annual World Economic Forum held in Davos, Switzerland, in which the main participants are business leaders. Eligibility depends on representing a company or financial institution that has sales of more than $700 million per year. It is at Davos, and less well-publicized similar occasions, that the priorities of global capital are articulated in relation to changing market conditions.

With respect to institutionalization, the main effort has been to liberalize global trade, reducing the significance of national frontiers and national economic policy. The General Agreement on Trade and Tariffs (GATT) negotiations have tried to establish a liberalizing dynamic, selectively negotiating away protectionist policies and prerogatives and pushing toward an integrated single market for the world, but in a manner that reflects the leverage of the North. A big step in the process of carrying this vision forward involved the establishment in Geneva of the World Trade Organization, which has an expanding mandate to override national efforts to place burdens on most internationally traded goods and services, but in a manner that worsens the terms of trade for many poor countries in the South.

The global governance framework that is emerging is seeking to implement a conception of the future that is responsive to the geopolitically managed logic of market forces.[12] Territorial states are contributing to this process to the extent that their political elites have been globalized to view their role as primarily one of carrying out the policies decreed by adherents of the economistic world picture.[13] Such a cumulative trend is not without resistance within leadership circles. The more geopolitically oriented elites, often associated with the more militarized sections of government bureaucracies and the armaments industry, continue to favor a conception of world order that emphasizes rivalry among leading states (and their allies); the importance of such traditional ideas as containment, deterrence, and balance of power; as well as the closely related academic fixation, especially in the United States, on "grand strategy."[14] This tension between the economistic and geopolitical world pictures is currently being worked out by the United States primarily with respect to its relationship with China, and to a lesser extent in relation to Europe, Japan, and Russia in the post–cold war absence of ideological tension.[15] In these settings, there is a renewed sense that despite globalization, territorially-oriented bases of political and military power remain crucial in working out the future of world order, but only on the basis of a dialectical interaction with economic considerations that are of a predominantly nonterritorial character.

Briefly, the effects of this rising economistic view of global governance are: (1) heavy investments in situations where the conditions are such that rapid and large returns on capital can be expected. (These investments have favored economic situations in which skilled labor exists but where workers do not have high expectations in terms of wages or unionized operations.) (2) Very impressive economic growth rates for an expanding number of countries in the Asia/Pacific area. However, these rates are subject to turbulent reversals, as revealed by the Asian financial crisis of 1997 and the years following. Economic growth has led to impressive alleviations of poverty, but also to predatory forms of labor abuse, a promiscuous disregard of environmental harm and disruptive social effects, and the emergence of new patterns of mass impoverishment. (3) A refusal to invest in those settings where the returns on capital were not positive, either because of political instability, an unskilled labor force, or high degrees of regulatory interference, factors that on balance have led to the disregard of most of sub-Saharan Africa and the Caribbean, as well as to selective deindustrialization in parts of the Global North. (4) As a consequence of the marketization of government policy, there has been a cumulative downward pressure on the provision of public goods (welfare, higher education, the arts, environmental protection) outside the area of military defense, which means that even when a national economy and its leading companies are doing extremely well, as exhibited by record profits and share prices on stock exchanges, there are few benefits for ordinary citizens, even those in the broad middle classes. Economic growth continues impressively, but the quality of life declines as people are increasingly squeezed in struggles to sustain their living standards and societal circumstances. (5) This atmosphere of diminished support for public goods is accentuated by a shift in fiscal orientation away from Keynesian ideas about deficit financing and demand creation and toward balanced budgets, deficit reduction, and monetarist approaches to economic policy. (6) In this atmosphere political support for *global* public goods (protection of the global commons, the United Nations, economic assistance for the South) falls away with adverse consequences, given the absence of either a supportive constituency or any significant perceived contribution by such public goods to the short-terms prospects of economic globalization. (7) The domestic political climate in the United States, the unquestioned global leader in this period, has taken a conservative turn that accentuates these tendencies adverse to social justice.

The Ideological Climate

These various tendencies, which are associated with the imprecise and slippery, yet indispensable, term globalization, have been accentuated by certain developments associated with the historical circumstances that exist in these closing years of the second millennium. The ending of the cold war provided a convenient occasion to discredit socialist and so-called "socialistic" ideological alternatives to capitalism. Indeed, the virtual disappearance of any serious socialist challenge has encouraged the architects of economic policy to believe that it is not politically necessary any longer to make concessions to the "dangerous classes."[16] This ideological circumstance is reinforced by two additional factors: (1) the postindustrial decline of the political leverage exerted by organized labor on government policy of democratic states and the convergent national electoral strategies of mainstream political parties, and (2) the widespread disillusionment of publics in the democracies of the Global North with an activist state, as well as criticisms of the excesses of the welfare state and a growing skepticism about the problem-solving capabilities of political leaders of states. In the background as well are the complementary attitudes associated with "netizens," the new militant political identities arising out of close affiliation with the Internet; political sensibilities that gravitate toward the ethos of self-adjusting systems; and a libertarian resistance to governmental regulation in any form. In relation to governance, the prevalence of such attitudes works against exhibitions of compassion for victims of globalization. Such exhibitions of social concern are resisted because they would seem to validate activist interventions by government to protect those who are being painfully marginalized by globalization.

Normative Results from the Perspective of Global Governance, or Why "Inhumane"?

To some extent, the preceding paragraphs explain why economic globalization, while clearly improving the material and social conditions of life for many millions, is still properly viewed as responsible for a dangerous momentum that is leading in the direction of "inhumane global governance." Four adverse normative effects will be stressed here, although there are others:

(1) Polarization and global apartheid: It is undeniable that globalization has fostered widening income and skill gaps, whether these are measured by class, region, gender, or race.[17] A crucial dimension of polarization is what some call the "digital divide," a term used to identify those who acquire the Internet skills needed for gainful access to the information age. This digital divide tends to accentuate the other, more familiar, dimensions of polarization. The contrast between the economic conditions, work skills, and political supremacy of Euro-American whites in the Global North and sub-Saharan African blacks in the Global South as situated at the two ends of the poles gives plausibility to the allegation that world order as now constituted bears a significant resemblance to apartheid as it functioned in South Africa during its period of racist governance, although there are some important differences as well.

This inflammatory contention of global apartheid also pertains to the flows of refugees and migrants, drugs, nuclear and other ultrahazardous wastes, and weapons, with the white Global North being ever more vigilant gatekeepers while the darker portions of the Global South become more and more looked upon as dumping grounds for whatever is unwanted by or dangerous for those who are prospering. It should also be noted that the affluence of the Euro-American North has not succeeded in diminishing either absolute or relative poverty.[18]

(2) Neglect of human suffering: This dynamic of polarization, even if separated from its racial and civilizational implications, is also destructive to an ethos of human solidarity and community, as it rationalizes the distinction between winners and losers, treating the range of outcomes as justifiable results of market operations and not occasions for remedial action. To the extent that the state becomes implicated in this outlook, there is a shift by stages from the compassionate to the cruel state, a social circumstance that recalls the earliest phases of the Industrial Revolution, when market logic reigned supreme and worker abuse was rampant, early nineteenth century conditions influentially depicted in Marx's critique of capitalism and also in the novels of such writers as Charles Dickens and Emile Zola. By neglecting vulnerable sectors of national, regional, and global society, globalization has the unintended side effect of creating forms of governance that are minimally motivated to act for the relief of human suffering. Of course, this trend should not be exaggerated. Government spending on social services, especially in Western Europe, remains close to historic highs. Actually, it is a change of mood and outlook—that is, of ideas—rather than a shift of resources that best captures the essence of the link between government and social wellbeing.[19]

(3) Decline of the global public good: Globalization, as accompanied by neoliberal economic outlooks, relies on private sector initiatives to uphold the claims of the public good. Such an orientation operates in various ways, including the social disempowerment of the state, by constraining its capacity to mobilize resources and by undermining public confidence in the willingness of political leaders to engage in disinterested action for the public good of their own citizenry. One expression of this disposition is the current effort to "downsize" the United Nations, while making sure that the organization does not challenge the

priorities of global capital. In this regard, to the extent that portions of the U.N. system earlier became oriented in favor of an overall ethos of global equalization, the right to development, and overall democratization, the organization was widely perceived in the North as an antagonist of globalization. Such a perception seemed confirmed by the tenor of U.N.-sponsored conferences on large global issues during the early 1990s, when transnational social forces (womens groups, human rights and environmental NGOs, peoples coalitions against Third World debt) challenged the market/statist coalition with ideas about governance that were premised on human solidarity, empathy with the marginalized, and a commitment to upholding the public good of all peoples in the world. The U.N. Social Summit of 1995, held in Copenhagen, tried in its way to place the social claims of people on the global agenda, thereby seeming to reject the economistic world picture as the wave of the future.[20]

Such events engendered a backlash within the United Nations led by its dominant members, and gave rise to reforms that would remove or drastically downgrade U.N. activities regarded as hostile to market forces. "Downsizing" was less about money than about this restructuring of the organization to satisfy the demands of the guardians of globalization and to ensure that the United Nations operates primarily as a vehicle for neoliberal ideas and relies mainly on the market-oriented Bretton Woods institutions (that is, the World Bank and IMF) when it comes to the economic matters. Significantly, the World Trade Organization was deliberately located outside the formal organizational network comprising the U.N. system. In part, this was a concession to the anti-U.N. mood prevailing in the U.S. Congress. Beyond this the United Nations is seen as selectively and potentially useful to implement global security in situations of the sort vividly prefigured in the Gulf War of 1991. Later developments, starting with Somalia (1993) and culminating in the NATO War over Kosovo (1999), cast doubt on the future of the United Nations even in peacekeeping.

What has been said about the United Nations also extends to the efforts to protect the global commons. Already, at the Earth Summit in Rio (1992), there was an effort to subordinate the environmental movement to the guiding role of the market. Maurice Strong, eminent banker, business executive, and secretary general of both the Stockholm and Rio United Nations conferences on the environment, made a thinly disguised move to give business effective control over the way in which environmental standards were to be implemented and articulated and even nurtured the grand illusion that business could be trusted to heed market signals in a sufficiently timely fashion to provide adequate environmental protection with only the most minimal reliance on institutional governance.[21] During the late 1990s, the U.N. secretary general, Kofi Annan, made a series of well-publicized overtures to the leaders of corporate globalization. His basic proposal, culminated in the Global Compact of 2000, was to induce multinational corporations to make a voluntary commitment to uphold international standards in relation to human rights, environment, and labor practices as an independent responsibility, that is, even if the territorial government did not itself impose such standards. These undertakings, dubbed by critics as "blue washing," while not yet fairly tested, did distract overall attention from this determined shift of emphasis in relation to global problem-solving from reliance on public sector initiative to encouragement of private sector solution. The voluntary character of Kofi Annan's approach to the implementation of international standards can be understood in this light as deference to private sector primacy in this era of economic globalization.

In effect, the social forces aligned to globalization were acting to ensure that governance structures responsive to the public good were contained if not rolled back. This required challenging certain democratizing tendencies that were moving the United Nations in an opposite direction and were giving the United Nations and other governance structures a stronger identity as agents of the global public good. This visionary undertaking was primarily delimited by transnational activist initiatives on behalf of the peoples of the world.[22] Such a confrontation can also be schematically simplified as an encounter between globalization from above (transnational corporations/banks/states) and globalization from below (transnational civic initiatives/women/indigenous peoples/human rights/environmental activists).[23]

(4) Looming technological horizons: Another complicating aspect of the current era is the emergent prospect of technologies with radical implications for human existence and the meaning of life. The human genome project, biotechnology, super-intelligent

machines, and menacing robots are all on the horizon and are being developed in response to private-sector priorities. The capacity to clone or fashion human genotypes, to identify "weak" and "strong" genetic traits, to construct "thinking" computers with super-human capabilities and sensitivities seems likely to confer upon technological innovators a role that far exceeds their regulative wisdom, posing great challenges to human survival and civilizational identity. In this sense, the problematic adjustment to nuclear weaponry within the public sector, where profits don't drive behavior to nearly the extent they do in the private sector, is a small foretaste of the challenges likely to face the next few generations.[24]

A Summary Assessment

These negative developments confront us with the likelihood that the third millennium will witness the fashioning of a durable form of inhumane governance that will pose severe risks of ecological and social catastrophe. Such an outcome is the latest, purest, and most ambitious phase of the fundamental application of the Enlightenment Project to human affairs: The continuous stream of technological innovations adapted to secularized political space in order to achieve the greatest material advantage for the owners of capital goods. To be sure, there are important contradictory tendencies evident and progressive varieties of resistance, described by the rubric globalization from below, but the political leverage of such forces is likely to remain limited to local battlegrounds and has the nuisance value of a global gadfly unless such dispositions are strengthened by religious commitments and by support from important sectors of the organized religious community. It is this possibility of a religiously grounded transnational movement for a just world order that in the end alone gives hope that humane global governance can become a reality, or at least an alternative future, sometime early in the twenty-first century.

Why Religion? Openings and Regressions

Among the surprises of the last several decades has been a multifaceted worldwide resurgence of religion as a potent force in human affairs, suggesting a relevance to the concerns of the public as well as the private sphere. From the perspective of humane governance, this religious resurgence has a double-coded message: portending the hopeful possibility and necessity of transcending the constraints of economistic secularism, which has become the signature of a disturbing interface between late modernity and a nihilistic postmodernity, but also simultaneously disclosing a range of regressions in the form of extreme variants of inhumane governance that arguably, in certain instances, make the repudiation of secularism a terrifying descent into political extremism as a prelude to repression and violence. On the negative side, I have in mind the regressive politics that religion has brought to such countries as Iran, Afghanistan, Algeria, and, to some extent, India and Sudan in recent years, but also the tragic and terrifying behavior of religious cults such as Heaven's Gate and Aum Shinrikyō, which have been seemingly incubated in the midst of secularized contemporary modernity.[25] Historically, then, it would appear that the outer limits of secularism are giving rise both to transformative possibilities that lead in the direction of humane governance and to regressive potentialities that mix in various ways the most severe deficiencies of premodernity with the most frightening sequels to modernity.

It is, of course, difficult to give an account of this religious resurgence that adequately situates it within the framework of the present, but this resurgence seems closely related to an exhaustion of the creative capacity of the secular sensibility, especially as it is embodied in the political domain. It is within this domain, of course, that modernity has been so closely associated with the preeminence of the territorial sovereign state.[26] Such a preeminence has been virtually unchallenged in this century with respect to the organization of governance in international society and is powerfully, if imperfectly, reinforced by nationalism, by far the strongest ideology of modern times.[27] Even the innovations associated with the establishment of the League of Nations and the United Nations were deeply rooted in a statist system of world order, and mainly represented extensions of statism that perpetuated the allocation of governance capabilities to territorial sovereigns, with the management of the whole entrusted to geopolitical arrangements that reflected the special governance role of leading states, what political scientists have called "hegemonic actors." In other words, a statist world order, although claiming to respect sovereign equality, was always based on a series of hierarchies, especially strong against weak, center versus periphery, Western or Eurocentric versus non-Western, and, most recently, North versus South.[28] It also presupposed the availability of war as a geopolitical instrument, despite a certain lip service given to restraints on the use of force in this century. But although this statist world order validated many patterns of abuse, either by way of immunizing domestic political order from scrutiny or through the interventionary and exploitative behavior of dominant states, it also gave rise to important normative ideas: limitations on the legitimate use of force, human rights, humanitarian intervention, asylum, criminal accountability of leaders. These normative ideas have been often subordinated to geopolitical manipulations of various sorts, but they provided some encouragement for liberal perspectives, which were imbued with the idea of progress in human affairs, and anticipated a gradual evolution of this statist world in the direction of peace and harmony. This approach to humane global governance is associated with the "democratic peace" hypothesis, which asserts that the spread of constitutional democracy brings an assurance of peaceful relations among democratic states, and thus if the whole world could be made to consist of nothing but democracies, then it would be a peaceful world, and if buttressed by an effective international law of human rights, it would fulfill the requirements of humane governance for the planet without requiring either disarmament or the centralization of political authority in international institutions.[29]

The world order difficulty with this approach to humane governance is that it neglects the social impact of economic globalization as enacted in an ideological climate shaped by neoliberalism. As earlier discussed, the overall cumulative impact of economic globalization, despite its positive aspects, is to predispose world order toward third millennium forms of inhumane global governance. And what is more, the influence of the economistic world picture upon governing political elites and the mainstream media is such as to condition and constrain the social roles of states. States, as now oriented, lack the will and capacity to safeguard their own autonomy, much less to fashion the ingredients of a just and peaceful world order. In this regard, it is notable that it is political elites that are most enthusiastic about institutionalizing the economistic worldview at regional and global levels as seen, for instance, in the political controversies associated with the World Trade Organization, North American Free Trade Agreement (NAFTA), and European Union, despite the fact that such advocacy means that significant governance responsibilities are transferred from the level of the state to incipient supranational actors. The European developments are the most dramatic in this respect, especially the relinquishment by European governments of national currencies. The establishment of a Euro zone, together with the suspension of border controls for intra-European travel, does move a long way toward creating a European identity as supplemental to the identity associated with citizenship in a particular state. Of course, for repressed nationalities, the prospect of a regional identity may be a partial escape route.

Expressing this interpretation in the context of this book, then, is a matter of understanding that the secular imagination is dependent upon the problem-solving capacities of the state, and that these have increasingly deferred to the main arenas of economistic authority (that is, World Economic Forum, G-7, WTO, etc.). One possible development, with relevance, is the degree of territorial backlash that might conceivably reverse this political energy and restore the role of the state as an autonomous source of authority, thereby rendering it potentially capable of creating a new social equilibrium between human needs/public goods and the logic of the market.[30] In the nineteenth century a kind of social equilibrium emerged out of the backlash against market-led industrialization, partly as an effort to co-opt, or at least moderate, working-class discontent. It was essentially a secular reaction that had its revolutionary expression in the Communist revolutionary movement spearheaded by Marxism/Leninism/Maoism, which was avowedly atheistic and aggressively antireligious, partly attributing acquiescence to an unjust social order to the otherworldliness of religious teaching and doctrine. Of course, there was an important insight in the assault on the role of religion, as religious institutions were generally aligned with ruling elites, and even otherwise radical religious leaders (e.g., Luther, Calvin) were at the same time characteristically hostile to the claims of the poor and of underclasses generally. But beneath this social line of criticism was the more fundamental spirit of modernity, with its search for truth in the realms of secular knowledge, illustrated here by the insistence of Marxists that their interpretations were based exclusively on social laws and that the resulting normative outlook was one of "*scientific* socialism," as contrasted with the visionary gropings of "utopian socialism," which were scorned as lacking in political relevance. That is, the acute social tensions of the early industrial revolution were addressed within the frame of modernity and secularism, with religion being regarded as either irrelevant or antagonistic.

In the present setting, revisioning of governance is by way of the market, and, to some extent, is reinforced by the self-organizing, globalist ethos of the digitized sensibility that shapes the Internet world picture. It is generally opposed to the social functions of government, to public goods, and to any deliberate effort to achieve humane governance. In opposition is the diverse transnational array of networks, coalitions, associations, and initiatives that has been earlier labeled as "globalization from below."[31] It is my contention that this early effort to construct a democratic global civil society is informed by religious and spiritual inspiration, and if it is to move from the margins of political reality to challenge entrenched constellations of power in a more serious way, it will have to acquire some of the characteristics and identity of a religious movement, including building connections with the emancipatory aspects of the great world religions.[32] Without religious identity, prospects for global humane governance appear to lack a credible social or political foundation, and, more important, lack the spiritual character that can mobilize and motivate on a basis that is potentially more powerful than what the market, secular reason, and varieties of nationalism have to offer.

What is meant by "religion" here requires considerable clarification in the course of constructing a global civil society and recasting the meaning of citizenship and democratic practice.[33] It is evident that religion cannot be reduced to any single religious tradition, although it can draw strength from the collaborative support of the various traditions, and that some aspects of certain religious traditions are antithetical, especially claims of being "the chosen people" or the exclusive or superior instruments of a divine or sacred design or of the enactment of some apocalyptic scenario for ascent to a higher form of existence. Such aspects of the overall religious heritage may authentically engage the lives and sensibilities of persons of genuine faith, but they offer nothing constructive in relation to the struggle to create patterns of humane global governance for all the peoples on earth.

From Religion—What?

Having identified forms of religious expression inimical to the quest for humane governance, let us now consider the potentially helpful contributions of religion. In setting forth these contributions, it is necessary that we allow considerable cultural space for a wide spectrum of interpretations of specific implications and that we acknowledge that humanist styles of thought are also capable of reaching parallel points of reference but lack the foundations of religion in the collective memories and experiences of peoples of varied backgrounds needed to arouse widespread adherence. The relevance of religion cannot be separated from its persistence in human consciousness and its role throughout history in the social construction of human nature. Religion is understood here as encompassing both the teachings and beliefs of organized religion and all spiritual outlooks that interpret the meaning of life by reference to faith in and commitment to that which cannot be explained by empirical science or sensory observation and is usually associated with an acceptance of the reality of the divine, the sacred, the transcendent, the mysterious, the ultimate.

The introduction to the complex matter of religious relevance offered here is intended only to be suggestive and is designed mainly to stimulate discussion, reflection, and dialogue on the positive roles of religion in the context of a global democratic movement for humane governance. A series of contributions by religion can be identified and listed, without elaboration at this point, and absent consideration of intercivilizational and intracivilizational variations:

- An appreciation of suffering: The religious impulse is strongly associated with a Gandhian acknowledgment of the "last man" (or woman), of the lowliest class, caste, race, and with a central commitment to lift up those who suffer acutely, a dedication to those most acutely victimized. It was Gandhi's insistence that politics be practiced so as, above all, to lift up persons at the bottom of the social, economic, and political hierarchy in society.
- Civilizational resonance: Whereas secular transformative thought tends to appeal mainly to alienated intellectuals, religious revolutionary language and aspirations have deep roots in popular culture and possess great mobilizing potential if activated at certain historical moments by charismatic individuals.
- An ethos of solidarity: Closely related is the unitive feature of religious consciousness, the oneness of the human family that gives rise to an ethos of human solidarity, and, with it, the sense of both the wholeness of human experience and the dignity of the individual. Such solidarity is a sign of religious inclusiveness and

celebration of religious diversity, contrasting with the narrow paths of intolerance traveled by exclusivist religiosity.
- Normative horizons: Responses to suffering and affirmation of human solidarity imply a belief in normative horizons that define human potentialities in an affirming and hopeful manner that contradicts and transcends present conditions, which neglect many forms of acute human suffering, tend to elevate the claims of the part or the fragment over those of the whole, and are fraught with consumerist and materialist preoccupations. Religiously oriented normative horizons converge in many respects with the humanist aspirations of a human rights culture.
- Faith and power: A belief in the transformative capacities of an idea that is sustained by spiritual energy lends itself to nonviolent forms of struggle and sacrifice, thereby challenging more secular views of human history as shaped primarily by governing elites, warfare, and a command over innovative military technology.
- Limits: A profound humility in relation to human thought and action that is sensitive to human fallibility, if not sin and evil, and appreciates the limited capacity of the inquiring mind to grasp the fullness of reality or to claim the truthfulness and correctness of any particular interpretation of what needs to be done in the world allows a person to remain open at all stages to dialogue with strangers and apparent adversaries, which can serve to correct mistakes, and to a sense of awe in face of the divine, which can protect humanity from idolatry.
- Identity: Identity can emerge from many sources and is existentially being reshaped by overlapping appeals to aspects of human nature and experience. However, the era of exclusive subjection to the expectations of loyalty to the state are being surpassed by both various modes of reexperiencing the deepening reality of the whole and by the increasing sense of the yet-unfulfilled future, an emphasis that can be highlighted by replacing the idea of "citizen" with that of "citizen pilgrim," a distinctly religious understanding of essential political identity by reference to a spiritual journey that is guided by the unseen and unlikely to be completed with the span of this lifetime but the value of which is an object of intense faith and dedication that encompasses traditional loyalties to nation and state but embraces temporal loyalties to a future that bring justice and peace to the entire human family.
- Reconciliation: Diverse ways of knowing are alternative respected means of coping with the effects of human finitude and

the impingement of limits, thereby diminishing the obstacles to a needed and desirable reconciliation of science, reason, and spirituality. Whether this reconciling process occurs within the domain of formal religion or without, or in both, is of secondary significance.

Religion and Humane Global Governance: A Concluding Observation

The perspective proposed is that a religious/spiritual orientation needs to be informed by the energies of globalization from below if it is to have any serious prospect of launching a political project that offers an alternative to that being foreshadowed and actualized by the largely economistic forces associated with globalization from above. It is not a matter of repudiating state or market but of insisting that these organizing arenas of authority and influence be spiritualized in accordance with the generalized attributes of religion. But it is also not expecting a miraculous rescue from above (deus ex machina), whether in the form of a sudden embrace of world government or the emergence of regional institutions and the United Nations as political actors no longer constrained by geopolitics and the reigning neoliberal world picture.

Humane global governance will only occur as the outcome of human struggle, and in this sense is similar to past efforts to overcome slavery, colonialism, and apartheid. Each of these struggles was substantially inspired by direct and indirect religious thought as embodied in the lives and works of devout adherents. Each undertaking seemed "impossible" at its point of origin given the array of social forces, fixed beliefs, and institutional supports affirmed by the conventional wisdom of the day to validate and uphold inhumane practices. In the recent past we have witnessed successful struggles against oppression carried on by the peoples of Eastern Europe and the Soviet Union, of many countries in Asia, and of the victims of apartheid in South Africa. They have enjoyed limited or overall success against great historical odds, although following through with humane patterns of reconstruction has not proved easy.

We do not know enough to conclude pessimistically that humane global governance is an impossibility. We do know enough to understand that such an outcome, if it occurs, will not come about spontaneously or without anguishing struggles, and that given the historical ascendancy of market forces and the widespread acceptance of the economistic world picture an alternative orientation can only hope to emerge if nurtured and guided by inclusive religious energies creatively adapted to the specific problems and concerns that exist at all levels of social reality.

The complexity and precariousness of a globalizing world is bringing into being an unprecedented degree of global governance. The forms of this governance cannot be understood by reference to the United Nations but are related above all to the efforts by market forces to coordinate and stabilize their operations on a regional and global basis. The extension of this type of global governance is threatening to human wellbeing and to the quality of social and political life at the level of the state. The religious challenge is to infuse the struggles of the peoples of the world for democracy, equity, and sustainability with a vision of human existence that is human-centered yet conscious of the relevance of the sacred and of mysteries beyond the grasp of reason and machines.

2.

Secularism in an Era of Globalization

> How to hold secure one's own moral and spiritual self, one's personal, reflexive destiny—amidst the crushing institutional forces of the state, but also of the marketplace and, yes, the church in its decidedly secular aspect?
>
> Robert Coles, *The Secular Mind*
>
> That a delicate shuttle should have woven together the heavens, industry, texts, souls and moral law—this remains uncanny, unthinkable, unseemly.
>
> Bruno Latour, *We Have Never Been Modern*

Points of Departure

Secularism is difficult to disentangle from kindred ideas of the "Enlightenment heritage," "modernity," "rationalism," and the "Age of Reason." There is about these widely used terms a shared sense of worldliness, of scientific method, and of suspicion about claims of transcendence and the sacred, and a refusal to be bound by tradition. Instead, there exists a belief in progress, in technological innovation, and in Western superiority and destiny. Secularism is also tied historically and ideologically to the fate of the sovereign state as the primary organizing unit of world order. Thus, at a moment when these keystone terms are all subject to doubt and controversy, the challenge of situating "secularism" in relation to religion, and otherwise, is indeed formidable.

The secular character of the state was an invention of Western Europe that took hold of the Western political imagination in the seventeenth century and emerged powerfully in response to specific historical factors. Secularism as an intellectual, and later ideological, current was, of course, a broader phenomenon than the ideological identity of the state. It was rooted in the desirability of grounding knowledge and the governance of society on nonreligious foundations of scientific rationality to the extent possible. As such, secularism and modernity can be compared with and contrasted to medievalism, which above all entailed the fusing of political and religious institutions and authority on the basis of faith in a shared transcendent and absolute truth. To the extent that modernity is itself now being partially superseded by a series of developments associated with "globalization," the status and nature of secularism are also being drawn into question from a variety of different angles.[1] The same sense of rupture can be expressed futuristically as well, often by deploying the terminology of postmodernism.[2]

Secularism as the foundation for the orientation of the modern state is intimately associated with the struggle to limit the impact of religion on the public order, but perhaps even more so to confine ecclesiastical influence to civil society. Religious warfare in Europe, culminating in the Thirty Years War, produced a broad political consensus that the state should not impose a particular unifying religion upon society. The state should become neutral with respect to the religious orientation of its population, and the ruler is obliged to uphold the freedom of conscience and belief of all citizens by adhering to an ethos of toleration.[3] In a genuine sense, the treaty protection of religious liberty marked, in effect, the Western origins of international human rights, and, although often not implemented in practice, at least provided a benchmark for assessing the behavior of states.

This secularist outcome was far from being a forgone conclusion, given the earlier widely shared assumption that the stability of a state, that is, the loyalty and obedience of the people within a given set of territorial limits, was crucially dependent on a sense of identity and solidarity arising from giving primacy to a particular branch of Christian faith and doctrine. Further, it had been widely believed that religious disunity in civil society would breed struggles by opposed tendencies to control the state and would almost certainly produce either oppression by the dominant religion or periodic civil war between rival religions seeking control over the state. This belief in the benefits of religious primacy based on the denominational affiliation of the ruler and the state provided the political rationale that underlay the maxim *cuius regio eius religio* (who rules, whose religion; that is, it is the ruler who determines the religion for a political community). Only after much turmoil was this ethos of religiously oriented states successfully challenged by the secularist alternative ushering in an era of religious tolerance.[4]

Some account must also be taken of the degree to which nationalism and patriotism moved into the vacuum created by this secularist rejection of religious identity for the state and its ruler, thereby paving the way for modern forms of mass warfare and interventionism.[5] Closely related to the secularist stance is the degree to which such states were particularly susceptible to "realist" world pictures of a fragmented humanity, in which the outer limits of community were coterminus with territorial boundaries.[6] The medieval world of the West was much more sensitive to the nonterritorial claims of Christendom and the identity flowing therefrom. With the recent rediscoveries of civilizational identity, especially in the face of the diminishing status of states, there is once more a widespread feeling of community that is larger than state and nation and linked to civilization and world religion, but still not so extended as to include the whole of humanity.[7]

The reliance on the idea of sovereignty to justify the concentration of power internally, and then later in relation to external actors, reinforced this view that the leaders of the state were accountable, if at all, only to their own citizenry when they acted internationally, and that war was discretionary for the sovereign state, subject only to the restraints of prudence and rationality.[8] It is only at the end of the nineteenth century that a slow process of providing a framework of law to regulate warfare began to take shape in the form of multilateral treaties. And only much later did any serious approach to external accountability gain political relevance. More recent initiatives, such as the Hague International Tribunal on War Crimes of the Former Yugoslavia, the campaign to establish a permanent international criminal court, and the attempted international prosecution in Spain of the former Chilean dictator, Augusto Pinochet, have intensified greatly this line of development. The indictment of Slobodan Milosevic in March 1999 for crimes in Bosnia and Kosovo, while he remained a sitting head of state, was a dramatic move in the direction of international accountability.[9]

A major concern of this chapter is to explore the impact of secularism upon political life, especially as it bears upon the changing and varied role of the state, which faces a range of contemporary challenges in differing civilizational circumstances. In essence, the nature of secularism as it evolved in Europe altered with changing societal settings, and it has also adapted to very disparate circumstances in the course of a series of borrowings by non-European countries during this century. There is, then, an interplay between the identification of several varieties of secularism through time and across space and the complementary inquiry into whether the secular state is resilient enough to cope with the deterritorializing challenges of globalization. If so, how will this affect our understanding of its character.[10] In effect, does secularism have a future in an increasingly globalized world?[11]

There is another aspect to this inquiry into the displacement of secularism. The emergence of international human rights in the course of the last several decades has imposed on governments a set of requirements to uphold religious freedom in accordance with notions of tolerance. In a sense, the traditional goals of secularism seem superfluous in relation to the old agenda of protecting religious pluralism or ensuring that the state is autonomous in relation to internal and external ecclesiastic authorities. At the same time, the virtues of "secularism" are very much being vigorously upheld in a number of countries currently confronting one or another form of religious nationalism or ethnic extremism; however, the focus of concern seems significantly different than the earlier European experience. It is less a matter of protecting the freedom of religion than it is of fearing the socially and politically oppressive impacts of a religious state that would use its coercive powers against those who were accused of violating religious orthodoxy in some way and were subject to punishment. In this respect, the typical adversary of such a non-Western religious state is not secularism as such but Westernization, marked by its decadence and its alleged destruction of indigenous traditions and identities, including those associated with religion, or, more specifically, with the "true religion." Iran in the first decade or so of its revolutionary existence typified this pattern but has now retreated somewhat, seeming to accept the view that to persist and flourish, an Islamic state must respect the diversity of beliefs among its citizenry and would not jeopardize its Islamic identity by embracing modern science and technology, despite their Western origins.[12] The reformist conviction is that Iran can benefit from modernity while retaining fully its Islamic character, thereby providing a new positive model of an Islamic state.

These themes inform the inquiry of this chapter: (1) the original adoption of secularism by the modern state in the West as it progressed internally from absolutism to constitutionalism and its mixed legacy; (2) a brief consideration of the dogmatically antireligious secularism of the Marxist/Leninist tradition; (3) the extensions of secularism to three non-Western countries that are mainly located outside the orbit of the Judeo-Christian tradition; (4) the pressures on the secular state arising from migration and capital flows that are characteristic of the current phase of globalization; (5) a short meditation on the uncertain future of the secular state as traditionally conceived; (6) finally, a plea for a reconstructed secularism that could also give rise either to a new kind of "compassionate state" or could facilitate "a world of regions." Either eventuality would centrally encourage the respiritualization of political life and reconnect the civic virtues of a regionalized and globalized citizenry with religious devotion and practice. This seems to be the most likely and hopeful next phase in world order.

The Initial West European Embrace of Secularism

It is difficult to separate the rise of the modern state in Europe from the adoption of a secular outlook by political leaders. As Ernst Cassirer and others have convincingly argued, the statist embrace of secularism did not by itself necessarily disclose an antireligious climate of fundamental ideas or popular opinions.[13] The story of the rise of the secular state is complicated, confusing, and somewhat contradictory, although the dominant trend is evident. The Peace of Westphalia, concluded in 1648, both brought the religious wars to an end and is generally treated as the starting point of the modern state system. The state then accepted the legal duty to protect religious freedom within its territory and pledged not to make war or engage in intervention against other states so as to impose a particular religion.

Secularism, in its central sense of worldliness and denial of transcendence, underlay this move in specifying the character of the state. The secularizing motivation was also associated at the time with several other related ideas: repudiating a destructive path of warfare associated with religiously based "holy war"; consolidating the authority of the centralized territorial state in relation to Rome, especially for Catholic countries; and minimizing the clerical or ecclesiastical role in the dynamics of government. But there were other tendencies abroad at the time that did link secularism to a repudiation of tradition and superstition, which were seen as elements of the medieval foreground inimical to the rise of commerce and, later, of industry. Along this path of repudiating earlier belief, the "modern mind" of empirical science and rationality emerged. Again, as Cassirer clearly shows, the concern was not with a rejection of beliefs associated with a religious mentality, which were generally affirmed by the seminal scientific minds that shaped the emergence of the modern. The main impulse was to remove religion from the social domain of public activity, where its influence was hopelessly intertwined with outmoded and constraining traditions associated with magic, taboos, rituals, inhibitions, superstitions, and the like.[14] Indeed, the major intellectual efforts to move toward modernity were careful to insist upon their acceptance of religious truth, even while the animating effort was to set forth new bases for thought and action that rested on reason and empirical methods of verification rather than revelation or faith.

The situation varied from country to country in Europe, making generalizations misleading. In France Enlightenment thinking of the eighteenth century definitely adopted an anticlerical outlook that was combined with the view that from a rational perspective religion as such was little more than an assemblage of superstitions organized to serve repressive and exploitative political structures. The French Revolution and its Napoleonic aftermath definitely initiated a crucial modern trend involving a transfer of political identity from religion to nationality. As religion was privatized, the public morality of the state was premised on nationalism, giving birth to a new fictive creature of the political imagination—the "nation-state." This new image of the basic building block of the post-Westphalian world was half descriptive, half myth. The notion of nation remains to this day deeply ambiguous, partaking both of the juridical power of the state to confer nationality and of the primordial sense of nationality arising from shared ethnic memories as confirmed by a common history, language, custom, and dress. Many contemporary tragedies and ongoing political struggles arise from these two meanings of nation coming into violent contention, especially when the primordial sense of nationality is awakened to challenge its submergence and abuse beneath the juridical claims of nationality.[15]

In the laudable effort to ensure an end to religious warfare and persecution, secularism as a posture toward reality incorporated several other features that have disturbing implications for the future. The first tendency was to associate a secularized public order with an amoral rationality that was devoid of spiritual, and even ethical, content. The modern state from an early stage invited into its midst a kind of technocratic sensibility that was purely instrumental in character and without moral scruple. This technocratic personality is manifest in such prototypic figures of recent times as Albert Speer, the top Nazi wartime administrator, and Robert McNamara, the American secretary of defense during the Vietnam era, men who served their respective states unconditionally on the basis of an extreme reliance on decontextualized reason, enabling the commission of massive crimes with a clear conscience.[16] In one sense, these two figures are not prototypic, as they were both haunted by their deeds, expressing partial remorse in elaborate and controversial detail.[17] Their admirers accept such apparent changes of heart at face value and commend their willingness to confront their past with a sense of moral concern. Their detractors are far more suspicious, regarding the retrospective look as designed mainly to achieve a kind of rehabilitation in the court of public opinion.

An intensified variation of this kind of rationalist outlook came to assert a dominant influence on the way those who ruled and represented the state conceived of the world. It shifted from the outlook of Niccolò Machiavelli, who entreated the prince to be unscrupulous as necessary in upholding the wellbeing of his city, to Thomas Hobbes, who incorporated the Newtonian view of force fields to portray the interplay of a world of sovereign states. Hobbes, who had translated the great classical work of Thucydides, believed that in the relations among states, power alone mattered, contrasting with the sort of civil society and community that could be internally established by a benevolent and effective government. In this crucial respect, the worldviews of Hobbes and Machiavelli are quite compatible, helping us grasp why the views of the former never fully displaced those of the latter. Hobbes portrayed the international setting as altogether lacking a societal character, making it incapable of providing a legal framework or even a code of comity and civility. In these respects, his outlook contrasts to Immanuel Kant, who articulated an evolutionary view of international relations as gradually assuming the shape of a humane and commercially guided global civil society.[18]

Of course, secularism as a posture did not necessitate such outcomes. Other possibilities were present, but within the historical circumstances of trying to free society more generally from the shackles of medievalism, the secular outlook tended to merge with certain epistemological and geopolitical tendencies. Among the paths not taken was the possibility of a more skeptical view of the role of logic and reason, an alternative depicted by Michel de Montaigne as opposed to the prevailing approach derived from René Descartes.[19]

Against such an inconclusive background, it is necessary to ground a contemporary consideration of "secularism." Should secularism be viewed primarily on its own in relation to the claim that worldliness is *sufficient* as a comprehensive posture toward reality? Or is it more helpful to recontextualize secularism in relation to religion as a means of acknowledging the religious character of the new scientific frontiers? And as a consequence to blur the boundaries between church and state, between public and private, between reason and faith? Or does secularism depend for its contemporary relevance upon freeing itself from its traditionally close identification with the sovereign state and its role? To achieve this result, and regain plausibility for secularism, would require a loosening of its link with the state, and expanding the view of political community so that it attributes far greater significance to regional and global bonds of solidarity.

Always lurking in the background is the realization that there are many secularisms reflecting the variety of distinctive settings within which the idea of religion becomes activated as part of an ongoing struggle over policy and practice. Secularism cannot acquire a settled meaning until the issue of the role of religion is resolved. So long as there is contention about this role, "secularists" will promote some view of the proper place of religion and "religionists" will challenge that view with claims of their own. In this central sense, secularism as an orientation toward reality is inherently embedded in the unfolding controversy and drama concerning both the meaning of human existence and the organization of the collective societal life of humanity.

The Marxist/Leninist Challenge to Liberal Secularism

The secular state was clearly capable of inhabiting a religious society, as the case of the United States exemplified in many ways. As is well-observed in the early nineteenth century by Alexis de Tocqueville, "[r]eligion in America takes no direct part in the government of society, but nevertheless it must be regarded as the foremost of the political institutions of that country."[20] Secularism has served well by separating church and state, allowing religious pluralism to flourish at the level of civil society, and yet keeping alive the relevance of religious ideals to political undertakings. But, arguably, such secularism also accommodated itself rather easily to reactionary social circumstances.

But there is one strong variant of secularism that moved from the same historical background to adopt an aggressively antireligious outlook, and that is, of course, the ideology and practice associated with Marxism/Leninism. With Marx's famous strictures against religion as "the opiate of the people," antirevolutionary effects, and the ultra-empirical embrace of atheism (what cannot be verified by scientific experiment as falsifiable does not exist), the position of Communist thought has illustrated the possibility of a radically antireligious potentiality present in the secularist demand that the state refrain from imposing any particular religion within its borders or beyond.

The strength of religious commitments among the Soviet peoples led Communist authorities to back off from the initial impulse to destroy the religious dimension of society. Indeed, some Marxist writing came to the point of acknowledging that religious faith can generate welcome commitments to achieve social justice, and movements in certain poor countries, especially in Latin America, adopted forms of "liberation theology" that incorporated many features of Marxism.[21] Often, too, the clerical exponents of the left were derided by their reactionary enemies as "red priests," and the like. Further, the veneration of Lenin in the Soviet Union definitely assumed a "religious" character, with chapels set aside and statues of the departed leader illuminated by soft light or even by candles. This kind of "secular fundamentalism" often led to the "return of the repressed" in surprising new guises and suggested the futility of seeking to stamp out religious belief by governmental decree.

Interestingly, in many countries of the South, governments were both secular and anti-Marxist/Leninist, both to avoid the challenge to the traditional civic roles of religion and even more so, to defend the existing social order and to avoid the sort of statist absolutism that seemed to accompany Communist rule.

Non-Western Adaptation of Secularism

Along with the acceptance of the statist model for political community, many non-Western states have self-consciously emphasized their secularist identity whereas some have not. Secularism, as such, functions more explicitly in these countries as a (sometimes contested) principle of order than it does currently in the West, where it is part of the cultural debate but is rarely invoked by political leaders or even articulated as directly relevant to controversies about public policy. Secularism for non-Western countries is deliberately borrowed from the West; it is not indigenous to such countries and as an artificial implant is not nearly as deeply rooted in the cultural life of such societies. Of course, it is adapted for specific ends, varying with context and over time. The issue is illustrated by a brief discussion of three cases where the rhetoric of secularism has been relied upon in political discourse.

Turkey

For Kemal Ataturk, the founder of the modern Turkish state and its continuing iconic figure, the initial state-building project, built on the ruins of the collapsed Ottoman Empire, rested on his perception of European states as success stories. Ataturk forged a Turkish identity by imposing Turkish nationality on all those who lived within the borders of the state, including the large, fragmented Kurdish minority, who possessed their own, separate language and cultural traditions. Secularism for Ataturk was seen as the key to modernity, and modernity was the path to prosperity and power. In the Turkish setting, secularism meant confining religious ideas and practices to the private domain and challenging even there the primacy of religious tradition. This challenge was expressed symbolically by forbidding men to wear the fez and by strongly supporting equality for women. In this regard, secularism became, for Turkey, synonymous with Kemalism, which itself became associated with a militarist state with rightist proclivities concealed behind a transparent constitutionalist facade. To this day the military intervenes in civic life to the extent necessary to preserve its secularist heritage, which is both anti-Marxist as well as anti-Islamic. This duality suggests that what is being erected is a domestic social structure and not just a wall against the exertion of Islamic influence in the public sphere. A particular aspect of this structure is the privileged role, status, and worldview of the Turkish army and its powerful allies in the private sector. The fact that Ataturk is a military hero as well as the founder of the Turkish state is undoubtedly important in grasping this particular enactment of secularism. But note that the anti-left side of Kemalism, so evident in the early 1980s, suggests that what it defended was not secularism as such but a social order that was potentially vulnerable to either left (secular) challenges, or to a resurgent Islam.

The Islamic political movement in Turkey has been careful to be outwardly respectful toward the Kemalist framework. The legacy of Ataturk is not challenged as such, despite his definite insistence on rejecting the sort of public role for Islam that it had enjoyed during the long period of Ottoman rule. At the same time, the Islamic political party offers Turkey an alternative to rightist secular rule, including greater attention to the needs of the poor, less corruption, closer ties to Islamic countries, and more permissiveness with respect to Islamic practices, such as women wearing scarves in such public spaces as universities and government offices. The perceived ineptitude and corruption of the mainstream Turkish political parties makes the present viable options for Turkey to be either indirect rule by the military or Islamic governance. That clash became evident during the brief reign of the Rafeh Party in the mid-1990s, culminating in the forced resignation, subsequent disqualification, and criminal indictment and conviction of its leader, Necmettin Erbakan, as a result of undisguised military pressure combined with a resurgent Kemalism in Turkish civil society.

"Secularism" currently functions in Turkey mainly as a code word for containing Islamic influence on the political life of society, including disallowing religiously oriented political parties from competing on a level playing field to gain access to state power. There are dangers for Turkey in such a course, including driving the Islamic political movement in more extremist and violent directions, or contrawise, paving the road leading to ultra-nationalist right wing political ascendancy or even a direct intrusion of the military. It should be remembered that a bloody civil war in Algeria occurred when the leadership of the state, with military backing, refused to give the Islamic Salvation Front (FIS) the fruits of its 1992 electoral success, which had been achieved by playing by the rules of the constitutional game. Of course, Turkey is not Algeria. The conditions are very different, but still the Algerian case should be carefully studied by those who now seem to favor what might be described as a suppressive secularism.

Iran under the Pahlavis

The Iranian case is illustrative of the failure of the Turkish approach to secularism and can also be invoked by those who support the Algerian refusal to allow an Islamic political party to seize the reins of state power. When the Reza Shah took power in Iran in 1925 he was influenced by the Ataturk model and faced a comparable challenge of building a modern state on the ruins of an old and great imperial dynasty without turning the country and its wealth over to foreign interests. Unlike Ataturk, the legacy of Reza Shah was far weaker, as was the military role, which was subordinated to palace rule during the long reign of the second Pahlavi shah, Mohammed Reza Shah. In a sense, the secularist commitment results in Iran seemed more successful than those in Turkey: rapid modernization due to high oil revenues, friendly relations with neighboring states, an ambitious reform program ("the white revolution"), a huge modern military establishment, a well-trained state security apparatus (Savak), and a close, supportive relationship with the United States.

But Iranian secularism turned out to be far more vulnerable to internal challenge. Unlike Turkey, the state remained royalist and thus did not even attempt to achieve modernist legitimacy by moving in the direction of political democracy. And it should be appreciated that the Pahlavi dynasty was upstart royalty without the traditionalist legitimacy of centuries enjoyed by the Ottomans. Arguably, without embracing constitutionalism, the possibilities of achieving a modern identity were much more remote, although Morocco succeeded under the capable leadership of King Hassan II. Also, the Shi'ite character of political Islam in Iran gave the clerical leaders a much more direct role and the sense of mission that they were reforming an unjust state, a sense activated by the Shah's moves against the property holdings and economic privileges enjoyed by the mosque, by the governmental failure to restrict the role of foreign business operations, and by the American military presence. The emergence of Ayatollah Khomeini in the late 1970s as a prime challenger to the dynastic rule of the Shah was a far more explicitly religiously oriented movement than what has emerged elsewhere, and it took the shape of a revolutionary struggle. Unlike Algeria, the Iranian revolutionary challenge remained generally nonviolent, despite widespread violence by the regime, until it achieved complete control of the state in early 1979.

The ideology of the Iranian revolution was directed against the secular Western ideas of modernism brought to the country by the Shah, the Shah's reliance on international capital, and his subordination to Washington. These ideas, especially the Shah's relationship with the United States and Israel, were attacked as "satanic." Secularism was thus identified with the "foreign," "decadent," and "modern," as it was with a liberal political order that limited religious influence. Khomeini was a powerful symbol for Iranian recovery of tradition and independence as well as for the return of religion to a dominating role in the public sphere.

It remains uncertain as to whether the Iranian Revolution had always determined to achieve the establishment of Islamic government in Iran or whether this possibility came about later, in the aftermath of the revolution, when Khomeini and his followers saw new possibilities that they had not previously believed to exist. During the period of revolutionary turmoil, the goals of the revolution were obscure, and it was widely assumed that the successor Iranian state would adopt a liberal secular constitution, but would also restore Islam to its former influential role in society. Currently, with more moderate tendencies expressed via impressive democratic elections since 1997, the present leader, President Mohammed Khatami, expresses many secular virtues: moderation, support for science and technology, and a commitment to normal diplomatic relations with non-Islamic states, including the United States. And yet, of course, Iran retains the structure and many of the practices of a theocratic state that rejects as immoral and unacceptable the idea that religion should be confined to civil society and private domains and that the state should not be itself Islamic in character. Clerical leaders continue to dominate all branches of government, religious dress codes remain in force, and the Sharia law governs. But can we call such a state less legitimate and democratic than many of its determined "secular" authoritarian neighbors? Or more "fundamentalist" than such a state as Saudi Arabia, which has not experienced censure by leading Western governments? Geopolitics seems more important than the repudiation of secularism in forming hostile and friendly alignments among states and in relation to the West.

India

The role of secularism in contemporary India has also undergone an evolution since Indian independence in 1947. The main role of secularism in India has been to assure the large Muslim minority that their rights would be upheld in a predominantly Hindu country. Secularism had less to do, in other words, with avoiding a religious orientation within the state than it does with ensuring social peace in a highly pluralistic and volatile society. The ascent to power of the Bharatiya Janata Party (BJP) in recent years has not essentially challenged this identity of the Indian state. Hinduism doesn't have a clerical tradition in the Western sense, and there is no history of religious rule in India, partly no doubt because the caste system deliberately separates power and wealth from religious guidance in a rather definitive manner. At the same time, Hindu nationalism poses a threat to Muslim and other religious minorities in India.

The deeper tension in India was resolved by Jawaharlal Nehru's essentially modernizing state, which was modeled on the West. This was adopted in preference to the revival of a traditional India, which would have looked inward and backward and was favored by Gandhi. Nehru was viewed as "secular" while Gandhi was regarded as "spiritual." But significantly, even Nehru projected an India that was morally sensitive in a manner that was quite alien to Western styles of statecraft. Nehru's secularism, which was pronounced in certain respects, did not preclude a strong sense of normative identity for India as nonaligned, as antinuclear, and as in solidarity with the Third World. Ironically, this kind of Indian moral exceptionalism has been undermined by the BJP decision to test and acquire nuclear weaponry. It was not that this 1998 decision was wrong, given the way states pursued their security interests in the world. It is that Indian nuclearism, besides posing serious regional dangers, deprives India of its antinuclear critical voice. Admittedly, relying on such a voice for many years achieved little, if anything, by way of disarmament, and yet it did give India a certain moral stature in international society that has been forever compromised by this embrace of nuclearist "normalcy."

A Note of Comparison

For each of these non-Western countries, a turn to secularism or to the indigenous religion was closely related to the magnetic pull of Westernization and its antithesis, an extreme revulsion of the West, its values, and its hegemonic tendencies. In Turkey, secularism is the antithesis of tradition, which is embodied most purely and comprehensively in Islam. Put simplistically, the modern Turk wants no part of what it means to be distinctively Turkish. It had to do also with imitation and denial of indigenous identity.[22] In Iran, this assault on tradition never gained the ideological backing of the elite nor did it become associated with the viability of state power. As such, Westernization was challenged and repudiated, at least temporarily, and tradition rigidly reimposed under the aegis of a religious state. During the most recent phase, the Khatami period, there has been a tension between rigid traditionalists and those reformers that seek the benefits of modernity. Yet these two groups have found common ground on a continuing rejection of Western style secularism and its accompanying repudiation of religious influence in the public sphere of governance. For India, the story is different. Secularism never really challenged the strong indigenous culture, and Hindu nationalism never challenged modernity.

The Case of China

In the late 1990s the Chinese government cracked down on a religiously oriented challenge known as the Fulan Gong. To discredit the challenge it categorized the group as a "cult" rather than a "religion." Once an association is viewed as a cult it can be easily branded as "political," "extremist," and "terrorist." Its rights need not be respected, and its adherents are portrayed as deluded pawns in need of rescue.

What is of great interest is that despite decades of Marxist/Leninist/Maoist ideological indoctrination, the sensibility of Chinese civil society seems exceptionally receptive to a religiously oriented alternative view of life experience. The Fulan Gong is a somewhat shadowy reality, having been recently constituted by a Chinese thinker, Li Hongzhi, who now lives in New York and has been protected by the U.S. Government to the extent that requests for his extradition to face criminal charges have been resisted. The main elements of Fulan Gong consist of a mixture of quigong, traditional Chinese breathing and exercise practices, and ideas drawn from Buddhism and Taoism. The more mystical side of Fulan Gong is associated with its claim that it has control over cosmic forces so that the faithful can receive healing energies and supernatural powers. Mr. Li offers followers a profile of virtue—no drinking, smoking, drugs—and an organizational discipline that has exhibited a capacity to mobilize large numbers of followers for demonstrations against the policies of the Beijing government. These demonstrations took place amid an atmosphere of repression, including public humiliations and punishments reminiscent of Cultural Revolution days, but one now under an official aegis of government.

The Fulan Gong movement has spread rapidly among all strata of Chinese society, including officialdom. It occurs against a dual historical/cultural background. One strand is a long Chinese history of militant secret societies that mount powerful challenges against a given political order. Fulan Gong is evidently viewed by the Chinese establishment as a dangerous manifestation of such militancy. Another strand is the Fulan Gong's move away from the antimetaphysical orientation of both the Communist ideological traditions and the still-pervasive Confucian outlook, both of which confine reality to the material circumstances of lived experience. In a fundamental sense Confucianism invented "secularism" long before the West, especially if its most essential element is deemed to be a worldliness that rejects hypotheses about eternal life, heaven and hell, and related ideas about original sin, damnation, and salvation.

Fulan Gong may not persist or manage to challenge Beijing rule to any appreciable degree, but its great recruitment success with many millions of Chinese followers and the intensity of the regime reaction suggest the fragility of Chinese secularism. In this respect, the Fulan Gong should be understood as one side of this multisided religious resurgence that has become a more and more important part of the world picture in the course of the last two decades.

The Relevance of Globalization

Of course, globalization is an elusive background reality that can be interpreted from many different angles with important implications for the state and its role.[23] The problems of maintaining the liberal secular character of the state confront a series of difficulties that can only be hinted at here but deserve a full exploration.

One concern arises from the migration of peoples in a manner that mingles civilizations and brings tensions to civil society. Islam in the West has been one focal point, aggravated by the long Arab-Israeli conflict, by the Gulf War and its aftermath, and by the rise of international terrorism. The secular state in the West is itself often engaged in such a conflict, as is particularly the case in the United States. The idea of religious pluralism and tolerance also runs up against serious human rights concerns, as in relation to disputes in France and elsewhere about genital mutilation. As well, there are issues of religious liberty that seem to encroach on certain ideas of separation of church and state. For instance, should Islamic girls be allowed to wear scarves in French public schools? Should scarves be treated differently than other expressions of religious identity such as Christian crosses or Jewish stars?

The reality of globalization in its relation to secularism was an aspect of the Salman Rushdie incident. It was not just the death sentence and ransom put on Rushdie's life in response to his publication of *Satanic Verses* that generated an inevitable clash between the domestic public order systems of the Islamic Republic of Iran and Western secular countries. It was also the realization that the boundaries of the state were no longer very relevant. Rushdie had to remain underground for years in Britain despite the fact that his book was legal there and was indeed praised as an outstanding work of literature. At the same time, many among the large Muslim minority in Britain felt deeply offended by Rushdie's book and wished it to be banned from public circulation, as occurred in a series of countries including even Hindu India. There is no way, within a given state, to reconcile Western ideas about freedom of literary expression with Islamic ideas about respect for the dominant sentiments and militancy of the religious community. It is possible to suggest that by coming to the West, adherents of Islam must be willing to accept prevailing cultural values, including the Western form of secularism, but this is a weak argument given the economic and political pressures that often account for transnational migration, making it an essentially involuntary necessity. The challenge of accommodation is quite profound. The territorial state retains virtually unconditional internal authority on matters of social and cultural policy despite the pressures of a globalizing world. Adherence to human rights standards is one way of meeting the challenge of diversity, but these standards are unevenly implemented and subject to a wide range of interpretations. Even the openminded Iranian president, Mohammed Khatami, endorses such a territorially exclusivist outlook: "Every people has the right to its own understanding of human rights on the basis of its own culture and its own history."[24] Such a view implies (falsely) that the world is divided along ethnic/cultural lines rather than that it consists of multi-ethnic states. Of course, this tension can be softened by respect for minority rights within a framework of genuine constitutional democracy. But the idea that a state represents a "people," a "culture," and a particular "history" is a dangerous myth. At the same time, it is a countermyth that resists Western pretensions relating to the claim that its values have universal validity and applicability in accordance with its modes of interpretation. In a sense, Khatami is affirming self-determination for the peoples of non-Western states, but such an affirmation must then address the internal challenge of plural peoples, cultural memories, and histories.

There are also pressures upon the secular state that arise from the fragmentation effects of globalization and the reemergence of identity politics, which take the form of religious and ethnic extremism. Such a backlash is evident in this decade throughout the southern Balkans, in several parts of the former Soviet Union, and throughout South Asia. The outcome of the wars in Bosnia and Kosovo led to the establishment of de facto ethnic/religious states taking the place of the former secular state of Yugoslavia, which had been premised upon an ethos of tolerance as symbolized by high rates of intermarriage in Sarajevo. It is a downward spiral from this sense of merged ethnic/religious identity to "ethnic cleansing," one apparent in many parts of the world. These developments are by no means caused solely, or even mainly, by globalization. For instance, the horrifying developments in former Yugoslavia are more directly attributable to the end of the Cold War, the breakup of the Soviet Union, the emergence of ultranationalist Serb leadership in Belgrade, and the irresponsible actions of outside governments.

These wider trends toward religious resurgence, micronationalism, and ethnic moves for self-determination seem linked overall to the declining capacity of the state to function as a "nation-state," that is, to provide the basis for loyalty and patriotism.[25] Arjun Appadurai puts this issue of state decline in arresting language by observing that the state system "appears poorly equipped to deal with the interlinked diasporas of people and images that mark the here and now. Nation-states, as units in a complex interactive system, are not very likely to be the arbiters of the relationship between globality and modernity."[26] The relevance of secularism to this changing context of governance is difficult to assess, especially in light of cultural diversity, which is often reflected in varying ideas about church and state and religion and politics. To a significant extent secularism as a mediating orientation embodied in the modern state was a Western adaptation to a series of specific problems brought about by the combined impact of the deep cleavage between Catholics and Protestants, the classical Greek dualistic approach to problem-solving, and the convergent pressure to disencumber science from religious dogma (a dynamic dramatized through the ages by Galileo's historic encounter with the Roman Church). For many non-Western settings, there is a single dominant religion that is taken for granted as the basis of public morality, the idea of either/or dualism is culturally alien and unacceptable, and the compatibility of science and religion is not, and in many cases never was, an issue. Of course, such non-Western societies have other impinging issues bearing on minority rights, ethnic militancy, religious extremism, and an educational system ill-equipped to provide scientific training.

Thus, in a globalizing world the relevance of secularism seems limited. Many of its goals can be more directly and effectively pursued by way of international human rights and their specific application to problems of religious liberty, including the freedom of citizens to reject a religious identity for themselves. There are special concerns about the way in which a religious state handles a range of worldly matters, but whether the secular logic of strict separation is a useful approach seems very much in doubt. Even in the West, with civilizational diversity extending in many countries well beyond Christianity, and with Protestant/Catholic passions a matter of rather remote historical memory, it is questionable whether secularism remains the most socially acceptable way to reconcile religious and worldly concerns.

This doubt is reinforced by the tendency of the state to diminish its social activist role, given the current ideological impact of neoliberal globalization. Over the last two hundred years, capitalist states have exhibited a range of possible adjustments, ranging from the cruelty of early comprador capitalism, which was based purely on market forces, to the compassionate engagement of Scandinavian social democracy, which encompasses the wellbeing of the entire countries population. The neoliberal state, with its bias toward privatization, its repudiation of welfare policies and high rates of taxation, its vulnerability to international competition, its emphasis on fiscal discipline, and its downsizing of expenditures on nondefense public goods, is definitely pushing toward a mean-spirited recreation of the "cruel state."[27] With the defining role of the state related to the facilitation of efficient market participation, issues of human wellbeing are pushed into the background, although due to the realities of electoral accountability and various manifestations of political backlash, such concerns still remain rather high on the political agenda. In this context, secularism as such does not seem to address directly enough either the causes of human suffering and contemporary forms of alienation or the means of cure, nor does the state seem capable in the present setting of recreating itself as the "compassionate state." What seems more hopeful is the formation of a "compassionate region" or some kind of "global social contract" that is committed to the implementation of the full range of human rights, including economic and social rights, and would engender a new climate of postmodern religiosity that is ecologically sensitive and culturally inclusive. Whether the moves in Europe toward integration can be viewed as a transition to a compassionate regional polity is at this point little more than a hopeful possibility. Yet, these European developments are the most radical, innovative steps taken since the state system emerged in full force in the mid-seventeenth century.[28] It is intriguing to consider that Europe, which invented the state and state system, may also be the creative energy behind the first poststatal alternative. In this central respect, European regionalism is a far more serious world order experiment than is the United Nations. At no point has the United Nations been more than a "club of states," a convenient vehicle for implementing a geopolitic consensus.

Is There a Future for the Western Secular State?

Such an inquiry is distinct from the question "Is there a future for the state?" It focuses on the relevance of the secular dimension in which the cultural heterogeneity of the territorial space has increased greatly and where intra-Christian tensions have mostly abated, although not entirely.[29] There continues to be a need, perhaps greater than ever, for the state to ensure an ethos of toleration that is operative on a behavioral level, but the priority is now intercivilizational rather than intracivilizational. It is the public order challenge associated with the "clash of civilizations," including modern and traditional or indigenous civilizations, modifying Harvard political scientist Samuel Huntington's overwhelmingly geopolitical presentation of the clash. If the secular state is to revive its role under these altered circumstances of economic and cultural globalization, then it needs to turn its emphasis in the direction of intercivilizational relations, starting with dialogue aimed at grasping differences and uniformities and seeking pathways to compromise, diversity, and areas of agreed universality. Of course, civilizations themselves are experiencing internal tension, with many diverse and even contradictory tendencies, suggesting the relevance of intracivilizational reflection and self-criticism as well. Such a course of action is especially relevant in the West, which has so often projected its power to control, exploit, and even exterminate other civilizations during its history. These ventures have been fortified by both crusading religious and crusading secular attitudes, especially the conviction that Western beliefs and practices have universal validity. The controversy relating to the universality of human rights, despite their Western evolution, is one important formative battleground for such ideas.[30]

If secularism is to have a vital role to play in the future, then it needs to shift its focus in these directions, taking account of the new setting that is undermining the autonomy of the state as territorially and nationalistically conceived. It seems evident that such a reformulated secularism, which would be based on a blend of civilizational and species identity, would require a religious as well as an ethical/human rights foundation. Thus, a reformulated secularism for the twenty-first century might begin to disavow the traditional separations of religion and politics and instead explore the possibilities for their creative reunion. Such a reformation also corresponds with recent ontological trends, including developments at the frontiers of science that cannot be accounted for by the sort of rationality that has guided the pursuit of knowledge in the modern era.[31]

Conclusion: Toward a Reconstructed Secularism

Secularism has played a creative and profound role in achieving a relatively smooth transition from the realities of medieval Europe to modern Europe. Its most notable contribution was to promote and institutionalize an ethos of tolerance that greatly pacified the struggle within Christianity between Protestant and Catholic rulers and that opened the way for the rapid growth of science and industry. This secularist record of success was tied to the identity and primacy of the sovereign state as the dominant political actor on a global level. But secularism also generated, even in the West, a series of difficult problems: By privatizing religion, it tended to privilege a kind of technocratic rationality (reflecting an ill-informed and misleading polarization of science and religion) that removed ethical reflection from the implementation of governmental policy, especially in external domains (that is, foreign policy), where there was no accountability to the citizenry. This tendency was abetted by the embrace of a mobilizing nationalism and a cult of patriotism that put loyalty to the state on a "secular" basis instead of on religious identity. It became easy from the perspective of this type of European modern and rational state to validate warfare and imperialism as the spread of a superior civilization and to make such validation effective and ideologically arrogant via its dominance over the technologies of destruction and power projection. Such patterns persist even in the postcolonial world, casting doubt on whether the international legacy of the Western secularized state is of much benefit to the peoples of the world.[32]

Also, secularism, when adapted outside of Europe, especially as in the United States and Canada, contributed to a stable constitutional order when the cultural landscape was predominantly Christian but divided between Catholics and Protestants. But even in these favorable settings, the relationships to non-Christian religions, especially to indigenous peoples, was not at all guided by an ethos of toleration but rather animated by an essentially genocidal mentality of destruction and elimination. Even within the Christian framework, it required an enormous struggle for women and minority races to achieve some measure of individual and collective dignity, and the struggle goes on.

The borrowing of secularist orientations by non-Western societies must be seen in a very different light than their adaptation to societies where Christianity prevailed. In such settings, the motivations were different, either to repudiate religion in favor of modernity or to provide minority religions with the assurances that they would not be persecuted under the aegis of state power. Secularism was not, in such countries, trying to affirm the values of a particular religion while making sure that different doctrinal interpretations of its beliefs did not induce violence and strife. Such a role for secularism might have been adopted in certain Islamic countries where the Sunni/Shi'ia split is prominent, but it does not seem to have been an important factor. Instead, the secular state was deemed to be antireligious and promodern, the assumption being that the two projects were mutually exclusive. Thus, to encourage a modern state, as in Turkey or Iran, it was seen as necessary by its leaders to cast doubt on religious devoutness even in the private domain, putting religion on the defensive socially as well as politically, and to engender an unhealthy climate of immitation of Western life styles and values. Such a climate is vulnerable either to oppressive approaches toward indigenous traditions or to an extremist backlash by traditionalists.

Also, for many non-Western countries, the path to modernity was based on a cultural heritage that did not rest on the neat dualisms bestowed on the West by Greek thought. Such heritages emphasized the unity of opposites and the artificiality of separating religion and politics. Secularism as applied in the West rests on a strong epistemological foundation of dualistic thinking. It also incorporates an attitude toward reason and knowledge that introduces a dogmatism of its own based on the supposed access of reason and empirical observation to reality and truth. Stephen Toulmin and others have shown that this Cartesian strand of modern Western thought is partially a compensation for the loss of religious certitude arising from the "death of God."[33]

There is also the troubling question as to whether secularism has outlived its usefulness in the West, especially given some special problems posed by intensifying globalization and its fraternal twin, fragmentation. With the temporary eclipse of the state as a creative social actor, the state can no longer provide as satisfying a basis for political identity as when it was relatively more homogeneous and autonomous. Transnational ethnic, religious, civilizational, and ideological identities are of growing importance, and territorial affiliations seems generally less important. The secular state is being challenged by other models of the state, especially the ethnic or religious state, and by contentions that human rights and democracy, while affirmed, must be adjusted to reflect specific cultural circumstances.

Finally, the normative potential of the state has been seriously eroded by the neoliberal climate of opinion that has dominated governmental policy since the end of the Cold War. It seems doubtful that the secular state can again become the agency for compassion toward the weak and marginalized under these circumstances. For a variety of reasons, to the extent such a possibility exists, it is likely to depend on wider frameworks of political identification and governance, the most promising of which is the European Union. From this perspective, the most hopeful future seems based on the image of the "compassionate region," which would uphold the human rights of all its people, including those who are most marginal and disadvantaged. It is doubtful that secularism, with its mainly Western credentials and its problematic adoptions elsewhere, can be the main creative force in fashioning regionalism in different parts of the world. Far more plausible is a sense of civilizational unity based on generally shared memories, values, and metaphysical assumptions. Such a civilizational politics need not produce a Huntington "clash" scenario, except in those geographical settings where Western patterns of dominance persist. It is not surprising that the most severe clash of civilizations has occurred in an Islamic region that contains a large proportion of the world's oil reserves and is the site of struggle as to the identity of its spiritual capital, Jerusalem.

There is, finally, the possibility of "rethinking secularism" in the specific setting of given Western states. Here, at least, the heritage is relatively clear, and its contributions remain of great importance in the historical course of Western development. It is also true that secularism became unnecessarily fused with technocratic rationalism and political realism at the level of the state, and that these features can be and are "deconstructed" by various forms of critical thought. On such a basis, one can conceive of a reconstructed secularism as facilitating the revival of support in civil society for a new variant of the compassionate state, that is, not merely a rerun of social democracy or even the "Third Way" of British prime minister Tony Blair or head of the London School of Economics Anthony Giddens, but a genuinely new orientation of the state toward human wellbeing that takes into account the profound changes being wrought by globalization. As such, the undertaking of this reconstructed secularism would involve the extension of human rights based on an ethos of solidarity, which implies some *collaboration* between religion and politics and church and state, including a possible reversal of the tradition of *separation*.

At present, in many diverse settings, individuals and groups are rediscovering their core spirituality within and without the settings provided by institutional religion. Partly this rediscovery is prompted by the deterritorializing pressures of globalization, giving more and more people a stark choice between being rootless nomads and citizen pilgrims intent on a journey to a better future. This better future can be associated with "humane governance" for the planet, a process that calls into question the heritage of political violence and cultural exploitation and imagines a future community that celebrates diversity while affirming the solidarity of the human species.[34]

Another force undermining the metaphysical complacency of secularism derives from the pace and character of technological innovation. The prospect of human cloning, genetic transparency, super-intelligent machines, and sophisticated robots is rather daunting, especially considering the absence of suitable inhibitions and regulatory mechanisms and the generally libertarian outlook associated with it. If money, power, and novelty remain the driving forces shaping technological applications, the rise of "dangerous knowledge" is a virtual certainty. This menace will inspire profound and varied reflection on what it means to be human and stimulate a variety of reactions that offer spiritual (and pragmatic) justifications for placing limits on "the new." To the extent such a political reality takes shape, secularism as we have known it will seem *anachronistic*, and the religious underpinnings of future styles of governance will seem so *natural* as to be taken for granted. Such anticipations may appear unrealistic to the point of irrelevance at this moment, but history has strange ways of surprising us. It is inhabiting this space and time between a discouraging acknowledgment of hypermodernist global capitalism and the hopeful reemergence of a human-centered spirituality that gives such a mysterious and precarious tone to any sensitive assessment of future human prospects.[35]

3.

The Monotheistic Religions and Globalization

Preliminary Clarification

It seems important to attempt a clarification of "globalization" as a concept, because it is generally so widely used and yet so diversely understood. Globalization as one summary of the contemporary human condition at the end of the millennium also sets the stage for assessing the relevance of religion and the significance of the unexpected revival of religion as a political force in a variety of civilizational settings.[1] Perhaps the most fundamental aspect of globalization is the pervasive compression of time and space, affecting the way we think, feel, and act and introducing speed, proximity, and hybridity as defining attributes of our daily human experience. That is, history appears to be accelerating, as exemplified by the extraordinary velocity of innovation characteristic of information technology. As well, the visual presentation of world news, including even wars, in real time is abolishing our sense of distance, compacting space while intermingling virtuality with reality. Also, various categories of migration are creating hybrid cultural circumstances of multi-ethnicity. As such, our consciousness of reality is being radically configured by globalization in ways that we are only beginning to understand.

At a second level, closely intertwined with the first, is the transforming impact of information technology on the organization and functioning of the world, giving a centrality to the computer and the Internet as sources of power and wealth that epitomize a new era. This revolutionary control over information is also being used to create new patterns of dominance in economic, political, and cultural life. It is creating an impression, as in the 1999 NATO War against Serbia, of invincibility and total control, making if feasible for the side with superiority in informatics to wage war at minimum risk to itself.

At a third level, also linked, but less obviously, is the adoption of a series of ideas that validate a shift in governing style, a transfer of responsibility and authority from the state to the market, and that convert the state into an instrument to facilitate market forces. These ideas have been labeled "neoliberalism" and "Wall Street capitalism" to call attention to the priority being accorded the efficient use of capital to generate maximum growth and profits. There are a series of related policy moves that follow naturally from this perspective, including support for tax relief, privatization, liberalization, minimizing government regulation, downsizing social services, and endowing corporate and financial leadership with great influence. The basic idea is to subject government operations, to the extent possible, to the discipline of global capital, a logic that may or may not be consistent with the will of the electorate or the premises of constitutional democracy. If economic efficiency offers the best criterion of good government, then a citizenry that favors "social democracy" and a high budget for public goods (environment, education, health) will appear to be increasingly "dysfunctional." Such developments have profound implications for the nature of democracy, currently seen as the only "legitimate" form of government. An important link between these ideas and the technological revolution associated with the Internet is the libertarian bias toward "self-organizing systems." Such arrangements do not need any centralized guidance for their operations and are indeed distorted in their functioning by even good faith efforts to promote valued ends through intervention. In effect, globalization *as presently constituted* embodies a strong antiregulatory, anti-institutional, and antigovernmental set of attitudes.[2] Against this background the role of religion appears to be characteristically confusing and inconsistent. Mainstream religion in the West has tended to be a passive supporter of the evolution of modernity and the turn toward capitalism. But religion is also the most vibrant source of resistance to reductive views of human nature, especially those associated with materialism. Religion is centered upon a spiritual view of human nature and of the sacred character of life. As such, religion is challenged by the dominant motifs of globalization and by the associated technologies so closely associated with its stream of radical innovations. Either religion will disappear due to the challenge or it will reemerge as a force for renewal that offers resistance to neoliberal globalization and provides alternative readings of reality. The monotheistic religions are particularly challenged as their locus is within the West, where the rise of technological dynamism has culminated in what we are describing as "globalization."

The Complexities of the Religious Revival

For several centuries, especially in the West, as a consequence of the manner in which the modern state was formed, the most basic trend in public space resulted in increasing secularization and materialism with religion confined to the domain of private worship.[3] With the Enlightenment and accompanying scientific revolution, there arose the associated idea that human progress rested on applying reason to the conduct of human affairs to the greatest extent possible, primarily through the many achievements of technological innovation. From this perspective, religion appeared as a premodern legacy that was gradually becoming superfluous in relation to the evolution of the human condition and would in time be replaced by the scientific imagination that was (misleadingly) supposed to be inherently rationalistic and antireligious. In Friedrich Nietzsche's provocation, "God is dead!"

Such a sense of the weakening of religion was reinforced in the nineteenth century by Karl Marx's influential and complementary view that "religion was the opiate of the people." Religion from a Marxist perspective was a central feature of the paralyzing ideology of class rule, along with the Rule of Law, which inhibited the kind of revolutionary action that was alone capable of liberating societies from structures of exploitation and oppression. And indeed to the extent that Communism triumphed, religion was initially suppressed to the extent possible or, at best, barely tolerated. Beyond this, the vitality of capitalism was tied to consumerism and a latent materialism, extending far beyond human needs and artificially aroused by many billions spent annually on advertising.

In these respects, modernity, including the rival strategies of modernization that were at the core of the East/West conflict during the Cold War era, was directly correlated with the decline and marginalization of religion. The more modern a society, the less religious it should be, at least at the level of governance. Such a pattern of cultural evolution was also widely associated with Western hegemony, resting upon industrialization and its extension to war-waging technologies. Kemal Ataturk, the founder and inventor of Turkey in the aftermath of World War I, deliberately imitated this Western model of modernization as a preferred political path, including its corollary insistence on confining religion to the private sphere. This same pattern was soon afterwards adopted by the Pahlavi dynasty in Iran in its failed attempt to build national power and prosperity through the imitation of Western modernization, including a focus on secularization of education and cultural life. Of course, a repudiation of modernity in the name of religion creates severe problems of geopolitical isolation, economic viability, and civil unrest. The post-Khomeini reform movement epitomizes a reaction to such an adverse pattern.

In relation to modernity, the three monotheistic religions have had generally divergent experiences that bear upon their current interplay. Christianity, dominant in Europe and North America, led the way to modernity as well as projected its power globally, initially with religion serving as an instrument of and justification for colonial rule. It was within Christian Europe that capitalism took shape, with its encouragement of individual initiative and the work ethic, even if at the expense of community solidarity and religious devotion. Here, also, the coherence of society was fostered by a state-sponsored nationalism, creating the fiction of the nation-state, a political myth that was intended to encourage loyalty to the state and to overcome, or at least pacify, ethnic and religious differences. Indeed, nationalism in large part provided political rulers with a cohering ideology that took over such a role from religion and allowed the mobilization of a society for various undertakings, most notably, for war.

It was Christian Europe that also gave rise to clear formulations of the separation of church and state, later a cornerstone of constitutional democracies. Such separation was initially seen as a way of reducing the danger of religious warfare and ensuring religious minorities of nondiscrimination, thereby creating a climate of tolerance. Subsequently, the exclusion of religion from the governance of society was perceived as part of the process of secular evolution, creating a more rational and efficient state that was no longer beholden to outmoded traditions and premodern—and often anti-modern—authority structures.

The Judaic presence in Europe since Roman times was one of minority status and subordination verging on persecution. The ugly realities of recurrent anti-Semitism remained mainly latent in modern Europe but erupted in the French Dreyfuss Affair and reached their climax in the form of Nazi viciousness that culminated in the Holocaust. Jews struggled to survive and preserve their traditions while adapting to the modernizing world around them. Due to certain European discriminatory practices through the centuries that disallowed Jewish land ownership, Jews were deliberately urbanized, making them strategically placed to take full advantage of the emergent capitalist ethos. The Jewish presence in banking and financial life, as well as the Jewish commitment to education, created an influence that exceeded the Jews' numbers. But the persistence of anti-Semitism gave rise and impetus to the Zionist movement, which succeeded after World War II in converting the vague British promise of a Jewish homeland in Palestine (the Balfour Declaration) that had been made a generation earlier into the modern, secular, Westernized, yet ethnically delineated, state of Israel. The emergence of an independent Israel in 1948 set the stage for the still-unresolved Jewish/Islamic regional conflict that produced a series of wars in the Middle East. Despite this modernity, the foundational aspiration to establish an ethnically distinct "Jewish state" was an indirect challenge to the legitimizing notion of ethnic and religious neutrality that had been a defining characteristic of the modern European state. It was also more frontally a direct challenge to the identity and wellbeing of the indigenous Palestinian population. This interreligious conflict has a material dimension with respect to land, dispossession, and self-determination for the Palestinians, but it has also a symbolic religious dimension that centers on the control over the holy city of Jerusalem. Over the course of time, as well, Israel has, to an extent, become desecularized due to the rising influence of Orthodox Judaism and of religious parties while continuously more modern with respect to its economy and military capabilities.

In this historical dynamic, Islam was both dormant and victimized. The Christian crusades marked the effort of Christian Europe to roll back the Muslim challenge once and for all. As colonialism spread to the Islamic world, especially after the Ottoman collapse early in the twentieth century, the mosque often became a place of refuge and resistance, preserving identity and tradition. Yet, such a role also meant a reluctance to pursue the path of modernization.

As Ataturk's challenge to Islam suggests and the Turkish experience exemplifies, there was a tension between Islam and modernity. This circumstance was accentuated in this century by the discovery of enormous oil deposits in Islamic countries and the role of oil in promoting economic growth for the colonial powers. The establishment of Israel was also a turning point, reinforcing the Islamic sense of victimization and creating a violent encounter with Zionist aspirations and Western geopolitical alignments, thereby reversing centuries of relatively harmonious coexistence that compared very favorably to the Jewish/Christian interaction.

This selective sketch of historical background highlights the problematic aspects of the relations among the monotheistic religions and the extent to which religion and politics have been either fused or split. The basic conditioning factors can be summarized as follows:

- The Christian West split religion from politics to achieve social peace and as a byproduct gained economic and military ascendancy.
- The Islamic world fused religion and politics in its struggle to maintain identity but endured decline and domination, only recently reasserting its civilizational autonomy.
- The Jewish people endured the Diaspora in subordinated or assimilated circumstances until traumatic historical pressures facilitated the establishment of Israel.

Of course, such generalizations are crude approximations and overlook the crucial internal tensions and subtle differences of belief and practice within each of these world religions. There are many nuances overlooked. The Islamic world had a diverse experience of colonial rule, with the non-Arab countries of South Asia less embattled. Europe was threatened at an earlier stage by Islamic conquests and expansionism, leading its aggressiveness toward the Arab world to appear "defensive" and "reactive." There are many divergent ways to interpret the overall political relationship that evolved among the monotheistic religions, especially in the Mediterranean region.

Such an account provides the backdrop for an inquiry into the present set of circumstances associated with a significantly higher degree of integration and interaction, thereby making the terminology of the "era of globalization" seem descriptive. Two factors dominate this emergent "postmodern" setting: (1) a global marketplace that is serviced by a global media controlled by the West and (2) an unexpected and complex primarily non-Western religious resurgence that challenges various aspects of secularization. This religious resurgence, which amounted to a reversal of expectations in many parts of the world, expresses tendencies that vary with their context. In some settings religious militancy seems mainly to be a backlash against the homogenizing impacts of globalization. In others this militancy functions as a mode of preserving identity and of asserting the interests of the poor. In still others it is a religious radicalism that fills a normative vacuum created by the failed radicalism of Marxism/Leninism. The revival of religion rescues many individuals from materialism. It is also spurred by the disclosures about serious environmental dangers of global scope. Religion has become more intellectually respectable as scientific knowledge has come to appreciate its own limited comprehension of reality. In these respects, the combination of apocalyptic fears about human survival and the rediscovery of the mysterious depths of nature and reality provides the cultural foundations for the reincorporation of religion without any implied abandonment of economic development or indifference to improving technological capacity.

The religious resurgence can take very different forms. In the Western popular mind, the resurgence of religion is often seen in alarmist terms as fanaticism and "fundamentalism." This awareness was given its full expression in the early phases of the Iranian Revolution, especially during the hostage crisis in Tehran at the end of the 1970s. This incident was widely interpreted at the time as committing Islam to a struggle-unto-death against the West and was treated in the West as a criminal challenge based on an explicit recourse to international terrorism. There is no doubt that each of the monotheistic religions has exclusivist potentialities that allow, or even encourage, its adherents to claim a unique and privileged access to truth. This characteristic decisively distinguishes these three religious traditions from others and creates an intracivilizational tension with the ethics and politics of human solidarity that underlie the secularist embrace of religious tolerance and, more generally, of human rights as specifying universal standards of behavior.

With the state becoming subordinated to the logic of global capital, many people have reacted by reemphasizing their traditional identities, including that of religion, and such a posture has often led to various counterhegemonic interpretations of the global situation.

Samuel Huntington's notorious "clash of civilizations" assessment gives a deterministic spin to these developments from a Western and hegemonic perspective, positing intercivilizational conflict and warfare as the inevitable wave of the future, which will give rise to an embattled West doing its best to withstand the challenges posed by Islamic and other non-Western peoples. In this scenario the West and Islam are pictured as locked in a mortal combat that can only be resolved by the defeat of one by the other. In some important sense, the resonance of the Huntington thesis arises from his recognition that the era of the sovereign states is past and that the future belongs to the political outcomes of this religious resurgence, which he associates with spatially distinct regions. This insight is diminished by his treatment of civilizations as geographic wholes, ignoring the important intermingling of civilizations that is itself a major byproduct of globalization. Huntington also neglects reconciliation possibilities, including the unifying impact of environmental and cultural challenges that are planetary in scale and the hybrid multicultural realities associated with intercivilizational migration patterns. The impact of globalization is contradictory, both generating a kind of homogenized world civilization that ignores civilizational particularities and revitalizing the traditional ethnic and religious identities that give renewed potency to civilizational categories. The homogenizing impact is partly decried by traditionalists and representative of the global South as a thinly disguised Western (or American) project for global hegemony. The backlash is decried by globalists as a descent into a self-defeating primitivism that hurts those who are currently most economically disadvantaged.

But, equally important, the new interest in religion is not properly associated only with the dangers arising from *exclusivist* proclivities. There are also important expressions of religious renewal that are *inclusivist* in various ways, including in reaction to the perceived menace of intercivilizational conflict. Many religious voices can be recently heard in these days advocating and arranging dialogue. There are increasing indications that religious leaders in various traditions perceive the Universal Declaration of Human Rights as compatible with their particular belief system and yet providing a series of shared commitments with other traditions of belief. These human rights standards, while subject to diverse cultural interpretation, provide the foundation for an acceptable and legitimate global discourse. So used, human rights could help fashion a climate favorable to interreligious solidarity. The Parliament of the World's

Religions, established in the early 1990s, has been based on the central idea that there is a shared core of values that unites the world religions and gives them a role to play in opposing both religious extremism and empty secularism. Hans Küng has been particularly active and influential in asserting the important roles of religion in terms of orienting political, social, and economic life around a "global ethic" based on an avowedly minimum, yet universalist, thin morality limited to the golden rule and the imperative to treat all persons humanely.[4] In a sense, this soft religious response itself constitutes a form of globalization that seeks to challenge capital-driven globalization on the basis of a more spiritual and ethical understanding of the human condition. In this regard, the world religions offer a potential countervailing force to capitalism that compensates for the removal of the socialist alternative from the political scene at the end of the Cold War. Historically, in the modern period of state capitalism, it was socialism, as politicized by the rise of an industrial labor movement, that challenged the market logic of early capitalism, which managed to produce a social bargain between business and society. This bargain neutralized the revolutionary challenge of workers by giving capitalism a human face in the form of the "welfare state" and its social democratic tenets of governance.

That is, there are essentially two divergent types of religious response to globalization, with many variations: The first response is essentially reactive, a backlash phenomenon associated with maintaining identity and redirecting the resources of society to assist the poor and forgotten. In this mode religion tends to see the nonreligious and adherents of other faiths, especially those associated with the West, as hostile, antagonistic threats. The world is thus hopelessly and dangerously fractured until the day when it is united under the aegis of the single true faith. The second response is essentially reconciling and encompassing, regarding religion as an aspect of a morally viable globalization that involves coming to terms with "difference," whether of a religious, ethnic, or cultural character, bringing concerns about equity and sustainability into play. Religion provides the foundation for a more compassionate and empathetic approach to suffering than is provided by economistic thinking, which is single-mindedly dedicated to efficiency, profits, growth, and ultra-individualism. In this view, religion also contains the only basis for the sort of long-term stewardship of the planet that is needed to avoid environmental decay and, at some point, ecological and, possibly, psychological catastrophe.[5]

Whether the monotheistic religions are truly distinct in their historical role from other world religions in this period of globalization is an open question. Certainly their shared history, intermingled peoples, and geographic proximity create tensions and bonds that enable a certain sense of shared understanding. As well, their common theological emphasis on one god as providing the source of meaning and salvation establishes a coherent and shared framework for theologically-oriented communication and may be helpful in some settings to enlist organized religion in the effort to soften some of the sharp edges of conflict. At the same time, many memories of abuse remain vivid, engendering specific fears and angers. The historical interrelatedness of these three religions has given rise to many disruptive struggles involving a suppression of heresy on the one side and a variety of secessionist moves on the other. Among the three monotheistic faiths, in the past, doctrinal strife, sectarianism, and misunderstanding have frequently generated and inflamed conflict. There is little evidence to show that the shared religious sensibility of monotheism provides a more united or more potent opposition to the shadow sides of globalization than is the case of the non-monotheistic religions. The polarizing reality of acute economic unevenness between classes, countries, and regions complicates any moves toward reconciliation. Also, it is arguable that despite the spread of Islam to South Asia, the monotheistic religions are essentially Western in origin, particularly in their truth claims, their relation to violence, and their trajectories of conquest. The wider orbit of world religions may have less of a common heritage. At the same time their outlooks are more easily attuned to meeting the challenges being posed by globalization, precisely because their interaction, to be meaningful, has had to be framed by reference to ethical and spiritual features that apply to all human beings and provide an organic basis for human solidarity. Unfortunately, the insistence on a separate religious identity for devout adherents of monotheism deprives the religious orientation of being able to offer an encompassing normative response to globalization, and thus appears to weaken efforts to confront these shadow sides of globalization.

Globalization and World Order

What is being understood as "globalization" is essentially a shorthand designation for a cumulative series of changes in the global setting of such magnitude as to modify our accepted imagery relied upon to depict the world. This standard imagery was built around the primacy of the territorial sovereign state as the only important political actor. If aggregated, the states as an assemblage constituted world order, with leading states playing a controversial role by providing a type of governance based on such notions as "balance of power," "spheres of influence," and "deterrence." This statist world order combined two distinct organizing principles. It possessed a *juridical* dimension, based on the idea of sovereign equality, and a *geopolitical* dimension, based on the operative impact of inequality and the fact that one or more states exercised preponderant power in a particular historical era.[6]

Globalization is complicating this two-part world picture in several ways. First of all, it suggests that an integrative process is taking place that affects the world as a whole, thereby superseding an understanding that international society is merely the sum of its separate sovereign parts. Second, globalization is principally associated with the rise of financial markets and financial and trade flows that are not subject to territorial control, making nonterritorial and "off-shore" arenas of policy and decision important. These arenas are not under the direct control of the state, which suggests that a description of the world as constituted by states is no longer accurate.

Third, both civil society and the private sector have become increasingly transnational in recent years, which accentuates the contention that a series of actors other than states are now playing influential roles with respect to the formation of international policy and norms. The Ottawa Treaty Prohibition on Anti-personnel Landmines (1997) and the Rome Treaty to Establish an International Criminal Court (1998) are illustrative of the political leverage and lawmaking impact that can be made under certain conditions by a timely collaboration between a coalition of NGOs and sympathetic governments. Fourth, the flows of money, ideas, drugs, arms, and, to a lesser extent, people around the world have eroded in crucial respects the importance of territorial boundaries. Fifth, the most prominent of international institutions, those comprising the United Nations System, were constructed in 1945 at a time of unquestioned dominance by states but now seem somewhat anachronistic to the extent that global civil society and the transnational private sector have no formal rights of participation or representation at the United Nations. Sixth, the results of decolonization have globalized the state system, but the global structures erected after World War II are Eurocentric, giving disproportionate status and roles to the countries and peoples inhabiting the Euro Atlantic region.

In effect, globalization calls attention to the main doubts about the persistence of the state system, although it does not necessarily spell its doom, and it certainly does not suggest the marginalization of the state as a political actor, especially in the domain of security. In most respects, it is more appropriate to consider how the role and outlook of the state is being conditioned and altered through the impact of globalization rather than to consider the era of the state as slipping into the past.[7] Nationalism remains the most popular force on the planet. Peoples without a state generally feel unrepresented or at least inadequately represented. Such peoples often claim a right of self-determination, including the right to form their own independent state. The territorial state, in the wake of the collapse of empires, is the only political form that exerts authority in a way that is fully acknowledged on the global level. States have actually extended their exercise of sovereignty in relation to the global commons by extending their coastal jurisdiction to include a 200-mile Exclusive Economic Zone and through their scientific and military activities in space.

The only area where the customary prominence of the state is in some doubt is Europe, which ironically was the birthplace of the state and the state system. European regionalism, especially since the implementation in January 1999 of the Maastricht commitment to establish a common currency and eventually a European financial architecture, does suggest the possibility, at least, of a regional alternative to the state as the primary organizing unit for human affairs. It is possible that if the European experiment proceeds further in the direction of creating a European polity this could spread to other regions and suggest a hybrid world order consisting of states, regions, and global institutions. With the diminished singularity of the state, in the light of the globalizing developments set forth above, it may become easier in the decades ahead for other innovative political forms to take shape. This dynamic has been identified by several international relations specialists as creating the prospect of a "new medievalism."

Within this *fluidity* as to political forms, *complexity* as to overall context, and *fragility* with regard to destabilizing developments, the reality of globalization is coming into being as a process.

A glimmering of these features of globalization was provided by the Asian financial crisis of 1997 and its wider repercussions in Japan, Russia, and Brazil. Most of the discussion of globalization concerns the impact of capital mobility, unregulated financial markets, transnational megamergers of corporations and banks, and institutional supports provided by the International Monetary Fund, World Bank, World Trade Organization, and others. These developments can be usefully comprehended as "globalization from above," being capital-driven and economistic in their ideological outlook.

But there is a second type of globalization that is also significant. It is a product of the activism of transnational social forces that are seeking to influence policy in specific domains such as environment, human rights, and development. It also represents an attempt to push forward the project to establish in credible form a set of networks and arenas that collectively justifies the term "global civil society." It is within this other globalization that the constructive efforts of religious activists to promote a global ethic are also properly situated. And it is here, too, that it makes sense to talk about a campaign to establish a viable form of global democracy, based on rights of participation in the global decision process and in moves to hold leaders accountable for acts done on behalf of states or other international actors.[8] Such a campaign is correlated with efforts to promote the democratization of state/society relations via multi-party free elections and constitutionalism. These two types of democratization are often in tension. For instance, the United States Government is at once the champion of democratization *for* states and the leading opponent of efforts to democratize *interstate* arenas of decision, such as those provided by the main organs of the United Nations.

In essence, this other, contrasting globalization is people-oriented and can be comprehended in gross terms by the idea of "globalization from below." It is important to avoid romanticizing this set of populist initiatives or to suppose that all "evil" is associated with globalization from above and "good" with globalization from below. The actual impacts are far too mixed to permit such a crude generalization. The transnational option is available to any civil society initiative and reflects all the contradictory outlooks present in modern society, thus including regressive undertakings as well as progressive ones. There is no assurance of any ideological coherence, even to the extent of compatibility with the promotion of a global ethic by the world religions, within this dynamic reality here called "globalization from below."

To the extent that the fall of the Soviet Union and the discrediting of a socialist alternative has socially disempowered the liberal democratic state during the 1990s, the rise of globalization from below may encourage governments and international institutions to act in a more compassionate manner, as in relation to debt relief and action to combat world poverty. The emergence of support for a global ethic and for a global democracy as projects for the world religions and transnational social movements may signal ideological resistance to the economistic emphasis associated with the current phase of globalization from above, which in the common parlance is all that is meant by "globalization." The same softening of a libertarian market-driven outlook is even being touted these days by leading private sector advocates, perhaps most notably by the currency trader and fiscal guru, George Soros, who has been issuing a series of warnings against the menace of "market fundamentalism."[9] The World Economic Forum in 1999 sought to deliver a similar message when it retreated from its unconditional endorsement of globalization and adopted as its theme the somewhat ill-defined notion of "responsible globality." Along the same lines are the calls by leaders such as Tony Blair and Gerhard Schröder for policies reflecting the "third way" and Bill Clinton's call for "globalization with a human face." Whether these moves are substantive as well as symbolic is uncertain at this stage, but debate about the shortcomings of and alternatives to neoliberal globalization are definitely in fashion now in contrast to the preceding several years.

The metaphors of "above" and "below" are relied upon to draw a basic distinction between initiatives undertaken by large organizations, whether governments or private sector actors, and those undertaken by people promoting their valued pursuits. This distinction offers only a partial preliminary means of sorting out the specific character of complexity that comprises the overall substance of globalization. It helps to focus our attention on a central encounter *within* the globalizing reality, thereby admitting the futility of challenging globalization itself.

Further analysis indicates many departures from this model, including coalitions of NGOs and governments on a variety of undertakings of mutual concern. Indeed, one interesting pattern that bears close analysis and monitoring is the formation of ad hoc coalitions as a way to overcome regressive positions of geopolitical leaders, illustrated above by the two efforts to ban landmines and to establish a permanent international criminal court. The opposition by the geopolitical leadership of the world (currently the United States and China) thereby suggests a new type of global political action that takes place on the diagonal between globalization from above and globalization from below.

A Concluding Observation

The future of globalization is very uncertain and will assert itself unevenly in different parts of the world. Likewise, the responses to its burdens and benefits will be diverse. The role of religion as a way of either confronting globalization, as in its most extreme manifestations, or of "humanizing" globalization by the advocacy of a global ethic is likely to remain important for the foreseeable future. Religious activists are also likely to play an important part in resisting those implications of globalizations that appear to produce suffering and distorted priorities, and thereby encourage various social forces to join together in building up global civil society along morally and spiritually sensitive lines. The prospects for creating some form of humane global governance in the twenty-first century seem likely to depend on whether the religious resurgence is able to provide the basis for a more socially and politically responsible form of globalization than what currently exists.

4.

Religion and Politics: Verging on the Postmodern

Future historians will certainly notice that ours has been a period of unexpected, varied, and multiple resurgence of religion as a political force.[1] This resurgence is not a universal phenomenon, but it is widespread and, in certain parts of the world, has become a dominant preoccupation of secular power-wielders. Whatever else is occurring, despite the continued ascendancy of science and technology, we are witnessing an extraordinary recovery of religious ways of understanding human experience.

To explore these developments, I propose to rely upon the following distinct, yet interpenetrated and contested designations of societal identity: premodern, modern, and postmodern. Such categorization is sweeping in its generalizing claims and can only be used in conjunction with an array of caveats and qualifications. Within the premodern are often pockets of modernist, and even postmodernist, anticipation. As well, the modern and postmodern contain remnants of the premodern. Premodern indigenous peoples, modern secular societies, and postmodern gropings coexist. There is, in other words, extraordinary unevenness of cultural circumstances through time and across space. Beyond this, the core perceptions of what such designations entail are bound to cover a broad spectrum and encompass a wide range of divergent realities.

Despite these difficulties, this categorization seems useful, even necessary, to gain insight into certain crucial macrohistorical tendencies that condition contemporary flows of events. The essential argument is that modernism is associated with the ascendancy of reason, science, and strategic forms of political organization as they emerged in Europe from the thirteenth through the seventeenth century and, finally, were complemented by the October Revolution in

Russia that brought state socialism into the world. Implicit in the dynamic of modernism was a process of Eurocentric globalization by way of colonialist extension and capitalist expansion. A strong feature of modernism was its basic secularism, a worldview that found meaning in the combination of materialistic and scientific developments, rendering knowledge and lived experience the equivalent of what an earlier age had regarded as faith and salvation.

The premodern, by contrast, was the condition of societies and consciousness prior to the conjoined predominance of reason, scientific technology, and state power. There were, of course, many variations on the premodern motif, including several that stressed community, hierarchy, tradition, and human dependence on higher forces of nature that were linked to a variety of pagan beliefs. For premodern societies, religion was indispensable to avoid a sense of arbitrary dependence on the caprice of nature and to endow life with meaning beyond the horizons of short life expectancies. The political leadership could sustain its legitimacy by upholding a claim to sustain sacred tradition as well as by providing security against external enemies and some degree of internal organization of material resources. Except under conditions of imperial rule, the separation of religion and politics was almost inconceivable in premodern experience. The struggle to achieve religious tolerance was an early feature of that experience, and the relative attainment of such tolerance was one important justification for modernism. When Jesus said "Render unto Caesar that which belongs to Caesar," the basic claim was one of religious autonomy purchased by way of secular deference. In an important respect, the Spanish Inquisition represented for the West the death rattle of premodern dispositions toward a state religion with totalitarian pretensions in the face of modernist impulses toward diversity, freedom, and the rejection of otherworldly orientations.

As modernism took hold, the place of religion tended to become marginalized. Religion remained useful for political leaders to invoke in certain modernist settings, but it was no longer at the heart of power or human fulfillment. At the core of political modernism was the capacity to mobilize economic forces and to wield destructive capabilities for warmaking purposes.

In the early twenty-first century, modernism retains control over traditional political domains, although with a growing number of exceptions. But there is something new unfolding that challenges modernism from without and within, what we will call "postmodern" as a way of describing some new orientations toward the nature of politics that are emerging to overcome the felt inadequacies of modernism. These postmodern moves are connected with the feeling that modernism no longer provides a credible basis for human meaning and species survival. One type of postmodernism is zealously antimodernist in sentiment, reasserting the centrality of literal and dogmatic readings of religious interpretations of human experience. The theocratic regime in Ayatollah Khomeini's Iran during the 1980's was a prime example. A dramatically different type of postmodernism is convinced that modernist dynamics are disastrously self-destructive and seeks to recreate a human future by introducing considerations of ecology and spirituality. Such postmodern emphases are often anti-ecclesiastical and nontheistic in their expression and belief while tapped into religious feelings by confirming the sacred and viewing human destiny primarily by reference to its nonmaterialistic spiritual aspects. Overlapping movements associated with ecojustice, ecofeminism, and spiritual self-realization are postmodern in their outlook and priorities.

The contemporary situation is confused by these cultural happenings. Some sectors of world society remain resolutely modernist. The success of several forms of religious politics challenge a major premise of modernism, and not necessarily in a liberating direction. Especially in the non-Western societies of Asia and Africa, the social impacts of religious influence on public policy have been overwhelmingly reactionary, often allied with operative centers of repressive state power and validating unjust and exploitative societal arrangements, especially toward women. On occasion extremist religious movements have provided a potent vehicle for the pursuit of self-determination and the resistance to alien rule. Only in Europe and parts of Latin America does one discern a consistent pattern of antimodernist religious outlooks that challenge the ethical and ecological shortcomings of modernism. This antimodernism can take many forms, but two are most relevant: (1) The main religious tradition can be reinterpreted to emphasize the mandate to liberate individuals and groups from exploitative arrangements (for instance, by way of liberation theology); or, (2) outside of formal religious traditions there can be a new overall interpretation of what life is about that goes beyond rationalist inquiry and derives significance from workings of and connections with nature and the cosmos (for instance, as expressed in various forms of "green politics," "deep ecology," and postmodern metaphysics).

The rise of postmodern religion as a challenge to modernism is, thus, not necessarily positive from a normative outlook. It may propose a postmodern "solution" that is fundamentalist or cultist in character and destructive of human potential.[2] Or, it may merely allow premodernist perspectives to be used repressively by those in control of the state and market.

But what is indisputable and of great macrohistorical significance is the worldwide loosening of the modernist grip on the political imagination.[3] This loosening challenges a linear understanding of history as moving in a single direction and opens up cultural space for a variety of new forms of politics that share the urge to counter the destructiveness and spiritual dryness of modernism and strive to provide the self and society with more satisfactory accounts of the proper goals of individual and collective existence. Such strivings also respond to the challenge of impending technological innovations that imperil the dignity and even the identity of the human species in a bewildering variety of respects.

The Changing Roles of Politics and Religion

Many of the confusions of the present age arise out of the reversal of roles associated with politics and religion: From politics we had come to expect revolutionary challenges to the established order and a mandate for far-reaching societal innovation; from religion we had expected consolation and community but no deep commitment to improving the public good of ordinary people in their everyday lives.

In Western liberal democracies, in fact, the separation of church and state has been largely celebrated for its contribution to the making of the modern world. This separation formalized the confinement of religion to the sphere of purely private concerns. Such constraint was intended to facilitate education and governmental efficiency as well as provide the basis for a unified and rational politics of state and society in the face of religious pluralism, thereby overcoming its heritage of devastating sectarian warfare, especially in the West. In the modern world, religious identity was declared irrelevant to the rational enterprise of educating the young, administering the political life of society, and unleashing market forces.

In Marxist-Leninist societies this process went even further, as the state took many steps to dominate the private sphere, as well—a comprehensive approach to control aptly labeled "totalitarian." Mainstream Marxist regimes of the Soviet era relegated religion to the domain of "superstition," a premodern impediment to the true basis for hope: material progress, dictatorship of the proletariat, elimination of class conflict, public ownership of the means of production, and beneficial application of science and technology to human affairs. Of course, the rigidities of communist ideology intruded on freedom of inquiry in a manner that resembled the most dogmatic religious orthodoxy, with crippling effects on economic and social initiatives. Beyond this, the reverence bestowed on Lenin assumed a religious aura and was nurtured by such religious rituals as candles and chapels set aside for worship of the departed leader.

East and West, during the Cold War, despite genuine differences concerning the role of private property and the market, as well as their contrasting views on the proper scope for individual conscience and political dissent, were in truth not far apart with regard to the societal status of religion. Although the West has taunted the East for its atheism, the West has itself "killed" God by denying the relevance of spiritual perspectives to the conduct of public affairs. The consumerist spirit of the West has been at least as materialistic in its way as the parallel insistence in the East on deifying the state and the bearers of communist ideology as the only legitimate objects of worship. Both East and West are antimetaphysical expressions of the modern project: to rest human prospects upon the expansion of productive efforts in this world and to rely on a continuous flow of technological innovations to make life better for a higher and higher proportion of humanity. In this regard, the former ideological debate between state planning and market allocation of resources is a tactical, intramural controversy carried on within the framework of modernist assumptions. Since the end of the Cold War and the related collapse of the Soviet bloc and the assimilation of China to the world capitalist order, it has been made to appear that the market has definitely demonstrated its superiority to the state as the vehicle for economic growth and efficiency, so much so that the metaphor the "end of history" gained temporary prominence. Further, with no ideological rival on the geopolitical horizon, the emptiness of Western materialism has become more apparent and has led to a process of civilizational adjustment. In this process, values other than material wellbeing receive greater attention, and religion and faith have gained more respect and salience in the public sector, particularly in the United States.

Until this comeback in recent years, organized religion, with notable exceptions, rather timidly adjusted to its diminished influence, especially in the West, where its institutional prerogatives were largely limited to the private sphere. In the Communist world, organized religion either acquiesced and became an enfeebled servant of state power or did its best to survive extreme coercive pressure that reflected the Marxist-Leninist dogma that religion is the "opiate of the people" and has no place in a revolutionary socialist society, especially given the relentless secularism of the modern project. Religion is an intrusion of the premodern, according to such thinking, that obstructs the true path of human liberation and is no longer needed as a comforter for those exploited by capitalist class denomination. The overall civilizational momentum seemed fully behind industrialism and the general conviction that modernization provided a universally valid solution to human torments connected with hardship and poverty. An extreme version of this view extended the hostile assessment of modernism to politics as well. In the extreme modernist society of tomorrow, it was hoped on some fronts at the interface of futurism and science fiction that the issues for political leaders to decide would be almost exclusively technical in character, mainly matters of allocating resources for purposes of efficient use, which would enable all important decisions by the state to be left in the hands (or heads) of technical experts, or better yet determined as the outcome of computerized procedures. Such an outlook welcomed the prospect of super-intelligent machines and sophisticated robots that would, in a matter of decades, according to some cyber gurus, displace human intelligence.

The appearance of politics (and politicians) in the wake of the disappearance of religion (and religious divines) was premised on the acceptance of efficiency and instrumental rationality as sufficient to minister to the totality of human needs in organized societal life. This technocratic optimism about human capacities to overcome scarcity and surmount the fragility of nature assumed extreme forms that seem ludicrous at this point. Herman Kahn, a respected futurist (besides being a notorious nuclearist), turned his formidable intellectual powers to what he conceived to be one of the greatest challenges likely to emerge from this triumphal scientism in the next century: the menace of boredom arising from an abundance of leisure time! In other words, this ultramaterialistic image of the future envisaged abundance replacing scarcity as the main challenge to societal leadership. Such views have reemerged in the early twenty-first century in a variety of biotech forms and posit the possibility of an obsolescent human species. Virtually any work, in this view, will be more successfully done by machines than by women and men.

In the course of the last twenty years, these circumstances have changed in a number of crucial respects. The inevitability of modernization has been openly opposed from diverse directions. Such opposition has had the common feature of reviving a sense that religion (along with politics) is somehow relevant to the defining issues of the current human situation. I will discuss two radically different forms of this change.

From one direction there has been a series of shifts within the religious domain calling for active participation by devout Catholics in struggles for liberation from oppressive economic, political, and cultural conditions. Especially in Latin America, priests and theologians have broken out of their roles as upholders of the established societal order and have impressively associated the mission of the church with an active involvement in overcoming the suffering of the poor. The liberationist perspective insists that the essence of religiosity is solidarity with the poor rather than attendance at church or the display of religious devotion through financial contributions. Even a nonprofessing Catholic who adheres to this liberationist view is given a better purchase on salvation than a professing Catholic who devotes his muscle or resources to an oppressive political order. Such an ecclesiastically shocking claim was bound to provoke reactions in the Vatican, as indeed it has. "Liberation theology" was the name given to these tendencies, which became especially prominent in Latin America during the 1970s, to emphasize the role of religion in the world, a role that was drawn, ironically, from the main nonreligious source of social and political radicalism—namely, Marxism—gaining an orientation appropriate to the practice of revolutionary politics. The sublime and surprising realization that religion, in order to rediscover its ground of vitality, needed to enter into coalition with its most determined ideological adversary has never been widely acknowledged or deeply reflected upon, much less appreciated, in the North. What is more, the receptivity of mainstream secular radicals to the participation of priests and theologians in their shared political enterprise represented a drastic reformulation by traditional revolutionaries and radical reformers as to the nature of their struggle. Such collaborations also implied an altered vision of the just society. In appreciating the magnitude of this double move, it helps to realize that religion had previously been treated as the implacable enemy and obstacle to revolutionary socialism as well as a source of resistance to it. Now, all at once, Christianity emerged as a revered ally of and engaged participant in transformative politics.

The mid-1970s triumph of the Sandinistas in Nicaragua represented the most significant fusion of Marxism and Christianity that gained state power in this period, leaving an ambiguous imprint in history. It remains even now such a troublesome phenomenon for conventional Western thought that its reality has been largely ignored, if not denied. Most American commentary on the Nicaraguan political system largely explained developments after the Somoza dictatorship by reference to familiar East-West categories: the government in Managua was labeled Marxist-Leninist and was portrayed as a Central American replica of Fidel Castro's more orthodox Cuba. For pragmatic reasons of credibility, liberals in this country generally failed to contest these assessments. Even those ardently opposed to helping the right wing contras were eager at the time (during the 1980s) to insulate themselves from accusations of Marxist sympathies or insufficient concern about Soviet strategic penetration in Central American affairs. Yet, dispassionate witnesses and commentators consistently noticed the real and persisting importance of religious convictions and vocation for the new leadership in Nicaragua. The Nicaraguan Foreign Minister, Miguel D'Escoto, one of four ordained priests among the top nine Sandinistas, requested a leave of absence during his tenure in a government constantly in crisis so that he might fast in protest against the extension by the U.S. Congress of further aid to the contras.[4]

Even if such an act is discounted as a gesture, it is a symbolically significant expression by a supposedly radical, Marxist-oriented political movement of its renewed willingness to join hands with those who find religion at the center of their personal and revolutionary being. Such a premodern form of political expression by a high government official alters the public understanding of political language, creatively implying the potency of nonviolent and religiously sanctified instruments of protest and resistance. One could hardly have imagined a comparable American government official making a response that so engaged his personal being and body, that so transgressed the established habits of secular and modern political life. Any comparable expression of religious conviction by an American government official would seem so utterly incomprehensible as to raise questions about sanity.

The U.S. Government steadfastly refused to acknowledge this religious component of the Nicaraguan experience, stressing instead the anti-Sandinista strain evident in the clerical hierarchy, especially as expressed by the Catholic leader, Miguel Obando y Bravo, one of the few Central American churchmen ever elevated to cardinal. By making such an elevation, the Vatican was unabashedly rewarding Obando y Bravo for his role in stemming the tide toward a reconciliation between Marxism and Christianity and was giving its institutional and ecclesiastical blessings to prelates who became active and partisan in their opposition to such threatening forms of radical politics. Not only the Vatican but the United States, for ideological reasons, did not wish to cope with a world in which Marxism and Christianity appeared allied in form and substance, preferring the familiar good/evil polarizations as a way of rationalizing its military intervention against the Sandinistas as a standard Cold War undertaking. If an American adversary was no longer godless, the United States government could no longer vindicate resorting to force through the presentation of itself as representing a fair and generous people who gained their own political independence after a harrowing armed struggle against a colonial adversary and were now acting to protect a neighboring people from a predatory, alien force.

Whatever we may wish, a Christian presence emerged at the center of radical opposition politics in many countries of the Third World during the latter stages of the Cold War. In South African townships it was generally religious leaders who gave direction and transcendent passion to the anti-apartheid movement. And Nelson Mandela, despite being a Marxist in his early political career, emerged from 27 years in South African jails with a distinctly religious political style that highlighted ideas of reconciliation and forgiveness.

In South Korea, also, it has been, along with students and workers, the Christian churches that have joined ranks with democratic forces and opposed a militantly anti-Communist governing coalition. And in the Philippines, many believe that it was the tilt in an anti-Marcos direction at the critical moment by Cardinal Sin, the highest figure of the Catholic Church, despite warnings from the Malacanang Palace in Manila that the Communists carrying on an armed struggle would benefit from the prodemocracy movement, that facilitated the triumph of the moderate, yet intensely populist, movement led by Corazon Aquino in 1986.

Significantly, ideological affinities gave way in this period to normative affinities: The Christian commitment, with exceptions, increasingly sided with the poor, without much consideration of global ideological implications. And political radicals reciprocated, generally welcoming and revering Christian leaders who joined their struggles, feeling validated by such an affirmation, and seeking to bridge from their side the gap between an emancipatory political vision and the progressive side of the religious tradition. Religious and revolutionary perspectives converged spontaneously to accord priority to a nationalist creed that aimed above all to wrest control over resources, culture, and the state from foreign and oppressive hands, and to transfer that control to authentic representatives of the people.

It is puzzling that this trend has not persisted in the decade or so since the end of the Cold War. Partly, the redemocratization of the major countries in Latin America have blurred the issues of reform and liberation. Partly, the strength of the market and the failures and frustrations of armed struggle have led to a virtual disappearance of revolutionary challenges in the western hemisphere, with the important current exception of Colombia. Whether liberation theology and revolutionary politics are regrouping under dark shadows cast by globalization is not clear at this point, but what has become evident is that the very visible partnership between religious orientation and political radicalism has disappeared from view in the early years of this new century.

It is not only in the Third World that such a constructive pattern of religion and political interpenetration has occurred. In Poland, the Solidarity Movement, although initiated by workers, was consistently inspired and protected by priests and officials belonging to the Catholic Church. The main Solidarity figures, including Lech Walesa, presented themselves all along as devout Catholics. Of course, the Polish Church has quite a conservative background with authoritarian affinities; its stance is part of a long battle against Soviet influence as well as a wider ideological fear of Communism. Yet, the Church was, possibly unwittingly, swept along in a political movement that was strongly anti-authoritarian and motivated by a democratic ethos that itself seems quite at variance with hierarchical and antidemocratic notions of authority long associated with the history of Catholic tradition and practice in Poland. In Afghanistan, too, religious traditions and leaders became a prominent aspect of popular nationalist resistance to Soviet encroachment. Unfortunately, in both Poland and Afghanistan, taking an extreme form in the latter, the victory over communism was followed by a reassertion of socially reactionary orientations on the part of the religious leadership. That is, bonding with nationalist resistance and against certain forms of oppression may be nothing more than a tactical and temporary stance by an embattled religious community, giving way when conditions change to an older, constraining traditionalism as an alternative to a supposedly morally permissive secularism.

Extending this survey to western Europe and the United States, one finds less focus yet a definite reassertion of religious presence on many political battlefields. In the peace movement, religious personalities were often at the forefront of opposition to militarist foreign policy during the Cold War decades, especially during the Vietnam era. In the United States in the 1980s, the Sanctuary Movement enlisted several hundred churches of all denominations, mainly in the southwest, to adopt a stand that challenged the primacy of state power in a crucial realm of public policy: control over the dynamics of immigration, especially deportation. The willingness of religious communities to extend protection in the form of "sanctuary" to "illegal" refugees from Central America, especially El Salvador, is impressive, given the prospects for prosecution and even imprisonment that confronted church activists.

A surprising number of Americans recently engaged in nuclear resistance during these same years. Many of these individuals, almost all formally religious, relied on Nuremberg notions of personal accountability to confirm and validate their insistence on a duty to disobey illegal state policy in war and peace, despite the probable consequence of criminal indictment and substantial time in jail. The main justification for such stands rested on an interpretation of citizenship and patriotism as centered upon moral conscience, but its underlying motivation was overwhelmingly a manifestation of a religious conviction, often worked out in the setting of a communal or semicommunal circle of believers. Adherents generally professed a radical version of Christian faith that sought, above all, to be attuned and responsive to actual and potential suffering in the world. In this critical respect, religion and radical politics converge on the idea of taking suffering seriously.[5]

Although the end of the Cold War, particularly in the United States, has resulted in a lessened sense of urgency and, with it, a decreased willingness of religious progressives to challenge governmental authority so widely and blatantly, the impulse to challenge persists. The agenda has shifted somewhat. In recent years, the most active focus of such religious energy has been directed against the imposition of economic sanctions upon Iraq, this due to the high human costs of the policy, particularly in relation to the suffering associated with economic globalization.[6]

As implied in the prior discussion, it would be a grave error to assume that all religious ventures in the political domain are motivated by progressive purposes or imagery. Quite the contrary. Reflecting despair and confusion, there has been a remarkable surge of extremist and narrow-minded religion in the last few decades. As argued in earlier chapters, the signs of extremism in religious practice are exclusivist truth claims and intolerance toward alternative belief systems. The most historically influential instance in this contemporary period is undoubtedly the first decade or so of the Islamic Revolution, led by Ayatollah Ruhullah Khomeini in Iran, although even it was less extreme than some other cases, such as the ongoing Taleban rule in Afghanistan that is particularly notable for its oppressive stance toward women. The Iran undertaking to banish alien modernism imported from Europe in favor of a restored, rigorous, theocratic polity shocked the Western secular sensibility while mobilizing many of its own poor and inspiring many throughout the Islamic world, especially among the youth.

The extremist appeal under the banner of Islam demonstrated a capacity to exact sustained and unqualified sacrifice for an indefinite period while offering no materialist inducements. When Iraq attacked Iran in 1980, a consensus among smart modernist analysts in the West anticipated a rapid and decisive Iraqi victory, underestimating the capacities of Khomeini's Iran to resist the superior military forces of Iraq as well as overestimating a technically superior Iraqi military machine to prevail on the battlefield against a determined adversary fighting on its homeland. The results were especially surprising in view of the substantial collapse of Iran's military capabilities, which had been developed by the Shah's regime in the course of the Islamic Revolution. The tidal wave of religious politics generated by the Islamic revolution at the end of the 1970s has been responsible for adding a destabilizing element to the political life of several Islamic countries, ranging from a brutal civil war in Algeria to antidemocratic suppressive moves by secular governments in such countries as Turkey and Egypt.

But it is important to underscore that the outbreak of religious extremism is not confined to Islam or to the Shi'ites in Iran. In Central America, for instance, evangelical and fundamentalist Christianity has flourished alongside liberation theology and has promoted a politics of deference to reactionary economic and political interests, including an acceptance of foreign economic and military intrusions on national independence. In Afghanistan, and less clearly in Poland as well, the positive role played by religion in shaping nationalist resistance must be balanced against serious reactionary aftereffects. And in many parts of Asia and Africa religious institutions have backed repressive governing structures, often giving a religious sanction to cruel practices of law enforcement. Such tendencies are evident in several Islamic countries, but also seem prominent in Buddhist Sri Lanka, where the religious establishment has consistently pushed the government in Colombo to adopt the most uncompromising policies on matters involving the rights and claims of the Tamil Hindu minority.

The appearance of American fundamentalists in the form of the "moral majority" evangelical Christianity and the "Christian right" has represented a determined assault on the lifestyle of secular modernity, especially as embodied in big cities. This Christian tidal wave has been generated by so-called "tele-evangelism." This sort of fundamentalism reconciles many Americans to their pessimistic expectation of nuclear or otherwise apocalyptic doom by converting a dread of catastrophe into the realization of a divine plan. The result is a "blessed assurance" of salvation, to quote one writer who was astonished by the widespread yearning for the rapture of Armageddon that she found in Amarillo, Texas, where the Pantex facility produces America's entire arsenal of nuclear bombs.[7] The AIDS epidemic has acted as a kind of objective confirmation of a radical religious critique of modernism, which has been charged with engendering a permissive ethos of private relations, especially in sexual relations. A repressive backlash of great potential fury and a renewed emphasis by politicians on "family values" have surfaced in the last decade or so under the aegis of the "religious right." The ugly expression of this backlash became manifest in the sudden rise of hate crimes, including unprovoked street violence against gays and minorities in America that is often passively tolerated, if not encouraged, by local police. Fortunately, the backlash induced its own reactions, including a mainstream emphasis on fighting hate crimes and legitimating diverse sexual orientations.

While awaiting the end of time, religious extremists are preoccupied with punishing the infidels—those who refuse to heed the true faith. Their harsh exclusivity fit well with earlier Cold War stereotypes of a Moscow enemy who embodied evil and was contrasted to the essential goodness and innocence of Americans. This moral dichotomy revived the Manichean heresy that envisioned the climax of history to be a war between forces of light and darkness, with victory eventually going to the former. The rejection of Manicheanism by the early Christian church was a consequence of its tendency to deny the presence of evil pertaining to those with true faith and, hence, effectively to deny the basic doctrine of original sin with its universal indwelling notion of evil. The Manichean claim was treated by the religious mainstream as a heretical manifestation of deadly pride, a fundamental vice for Christians since medieval times. It is ironic that the Cold War hardliners brought Manicheanism back into the churches in the guise of unremitting anti-Communism. Along with that shift, there has been a religious assertiveness on matters formerly secularized—for instance, the determined efforts to disallow prescribed prayer in the course of public education. In the early years of this new century, political leaders took great pains to acknowledge and manifest publicly their religious devotion.

How are we to interpret this tendency toward religious self-assertion, whether in a liberating or extremist mode? Is it coincidentally associated with various local circumstances of conflict and tension in the world? Or is a wider pattern of secular and modernist discontent inducing a variegated religious revival of global scope and indefinite duration? It was obviously partly a reflex directed at godless Communism and also a sign of desperation in Third World countries afflicted by poverty, corruption, and Westernization. Perhaps, for the West, the deepest religious challenge to secularism is soon likely to come from impending technological developments associated with cloning and super-machines, which throw into doubt what it means to be human.

My hypothesis is this: The complex modern project to apply science and technology to human problems has encountered several severe challenges that are undermining both its acceptability as a creed and its coherence as a basis for action. Simplistically put, modernism as practiced has given us nuclearism and is about to give us human cloning and smart robots, overwrought encounters between human activity and ecological viability, as well as a tattered social fabric. An extraordinary proportion of "modern" women and men suffer from acute forms of alienation. Normative and spiritual blinders have not served the human species well. Of course, the modernist logic continues to lure many of us with its promises to overcome *with* technology the difficulties that technology has created: belated modernization for the less advanced Third World countries, computerized democracy for those without libraries; missile defense for a country vulnerable to nuclear attack; unlimited medical capacity for the ills of body and mind. This crisis of modernism is generating nonmodernist responses as well. To cope successfully, we are urged by some to look backward (at heroic premodern antecedents) and by others to strive for a far greener future (heroic postmodern prospects). Both nostalgia and aspiration are emotive expressions of discontent with the instrumental modes of fulfillment associated with modernist solutions and realist horizons of expectation.

Religion provides the materials out of which to fashion either type of response and thereby to recast politics. Marxism—as a radical politics formerly attractive to the oppressed—has definitively failed to mobilize mass support in the cultural circumstances of Third World and non-Western societies and is now substantially discredited in most societies. Liberalism—as a moderate politics attractive to those with humane values and middle-class interests—cannot ground its convictions (which are generally little more than calculations) on terrain that is firm enough to support radical societal restructuring or normative risk-taking of any consequence. A religious radicalism has far greater mass appeal, especially given an overall disenchantment with the Soviet model of state control, the dismal experience of revolutionary guidance issued from Moscow, and the strength of corporate-led globalization. A religious grounding that deepens and extends struggle and enables mass forms of resistance that incur risks and accept sacrifices, insists upon an agenda of radical restructuring and yet does not abandon normative discipline.[8] The secular mentality tends to depersonalize suffering, whereas the religious mentality generally regards seriousness about suffering as central to its undertaking. Of course, religious extremism drives out modernists, but generally in a bloody manner.

Interpreting the Religious Awakening in the West

But the religious awakening in the West has another dimension. There is a reinterpretation of what religion is about and a basic, if rarely articulated, insistence that true religion is antithetical to institutionalization and hierarchy. In this respect, modernism is associated with the institutionalization of authentic religious experience transmitted from various premodern traditions. The growth of formalized religious establishments has also often meant a loss of spiritual vitality. Postmodern religiosity is associated with liberating spiritual interpretations of the human situation from all aspects of church dogmatics and bureaucratic practice. It may operate in a reformist mode by seeking to work within the ecclesiastical framework, or it may insist that appropriate religious activity can only flourish in deinstitutionalized settings that repudiate "structure."

Manifest in these postmodern strivings is an exciting new energy intent on remaking religion and, with it, politics, culture, and, above all, gender relations. Such remaking can either breathe life into inherited symbol systems by invoking a countertradition long marginalized by the mainstream or go back to a moment in the past prior to passage across some Rubicon of ecclesiastical and doctrinal decay. In Christianity, reference can be made to the Franciscan understanding of the sacred web of life or to the period of Christianity persecution, the long period of struggle and martyrdom before the conversion of Constantine. During these centuries, Christianity was pacifist, distrustful of political and economic power, and definitely in solidarity with the poor. This remaking of religion can also occur by weaving a new relational web of symbolic significance: by celebrating the arrival of a new goddess religion or a religion that is animistic without being pagan. The eventual doctrinal and institutional form of this religious remaking remains inchoate and diverse and is likely to remain marginal. There are many examples around the world of intense efforts to recover an unmediated religious understanding of life forces and a renewed sense of human purpose, although manifestations of this search are most notable in societies wrestling with the end of modernity.

This new sense of religion seems grounded in the earth (as distinct from descending out of the sky), is richly relational, and amounts to a return to the holistic sensibility of primitive, premodern tribalized societies. An influential passage from the inspirational anthropologist and neuro-ecologist Gregory Bateson's book captures the ethos that lies at the center of this new spirituality:

> What pattern connects the crab to the lobster and the orchid to the primrose and all four of them to me? And me to you? And all

six of us to the amoeba in one direction and to the backward schizophrenic in another? What is the pattern which connects all the living creatures?[9]

Another influential expression of postmodernist religion (and politics) is contained in a poem by Gary Snyder entitled "Revolution in the Revolution in the Revolution." Cleverly parodying Marxist-Maoist rhetoric about the drift of revolutionary energy, Snyder turns the secular rhetoric and sensibility of Communist ideologies in an unexpectedly ecological direction:

Revolutionary consciousness is to be found
Among the most ruthlessly exploited classes:
Animals, trees, water, air, grasses.

Snyder can be read as saying that the Marxists cut off their analysis of exploitation too soon and did not push their revolutionary fervor deep enough, into the earth itself. Or Snyder can be heard more cynically as dismissing Marxist materialism for the true revolution, that of the spirit, which includes giving our blessings to the whole of nature and finding power not in the Marxist way, from the barrel of a gun but, as he reveals later in the poem, from Buddhist meditation:

& Power
comes out of the seed-syllables of mantras.[10]

The new religious sensibility endows all of nature with a sacred, privileged status. The political implications are acknowledged and lead to new forms of struggle and activism in which modernist centralism, statism, scientism, and violence are under assault from a variety of postmodernist sources. It becomes worth dying for the sake of dolphins, whales, perhaps even on behalf of rivers, mountains, and forests.[11]

Illustrative is the *Rainbow Warrior* incident, in which French intelligence agents exploded two bombs on a Greenpeace ship while it was docked in Auckland, New Zealand on July 10, 1985, killing one of the activists. The ship and its multinational crew were seeking, on behalf of the earth and all its inhabitants, to protest and disrupt French nuclear testing in the Pacific Ocean. Recourse to political violence by France represented a modernist effort to destroy the postmodernist kind of transnational challenge on behalf of civil society being mounted by Greenpeace. It was clearly an act of war by modernism (as represented by the militarized state) against postmodernism (as represented by an unarmed voluntary association of green-oriented individuals). Most governments were silent in the face of French recourse to such a terrorist tactic. The explosions on the *Rainbow Warrior* released a swirl of contradictory statist emotions. After all, France was widely seen as properly upholding the primacy of the state in external relations, but it was doing so by committing an illicit and terroristic violation of the sovereign rights of a white, predominantly Western country (the violent deed was being done in New Zealand without official permission and in defiance of the country's antinuclear stance). Even governments hostile to the French insistence on nuclear weapons testing in the Pacific were discreet, possibly giving subconscious expression to a growing anxiety that the statist framework of international problem-solving was under siege. The interplay of forces released by the *Rainbow Warrior* affair suggests the continued dominance of the modernist framework of state power but also the vitality and legitimacy of the postmodernist impulse. The latter was eventually validated to a slight extent by an $8.1 million damage award issued after hearings under United Nations auspices before a panel of international law specialists.[12]

The results of this process were ambiguous and not satisfying overall. If the government of New Zealand had not been on record itself as antinuclear and had not felt itself as partly the object of the French attack, it is not clear that France would have acknowledged formally its liability for the damage caused. Even as it was, the damages awarded were offset in their legal effect to a certain extent by the agreement of the New Zealand government to release, for a fee, the French agents in its custody and allow French authorities to administer a brief period of nominal confinement. France may have been induced to pay ransom for its intelligence agents and, in this circumstance, to admit its own wrongdoing, but, in effect, the fact of this penalty is that the wronged party was a state (a modernist adversary) rather than a social movement (a postmodernist adversary).

The postmodern religious revisioning also takes flaky forms, for instance, by placing stress on the "harmonic convergence" of August 1987, which supposedly enabled the earth to obtain a "cleansing energy" from a rare alignment of planets. This alignment was supposedly of sufficient magnitude to overcome a period of catastrophic events otherwise predicted to transpire, according to several ancient calendars. Such "readings" of the cosmos assuredly express a kind of antimodernist backlash that do not lead members of society to enter the process of transformation in any serious or sustainable way. Gathering at sacred sites around the world at a given time may be exhilarating for the participants, and such activity possesses an irresistible potential for media hype, but it does not address the real issues of power, depravity, danger, suffering, and destruction in our world. Nor, I might add, do most of the New Age expressions of religious sentiment that promise their adherents growth and tenderness *in vacuo* or, what amounts to the same thing, on sunny beaches and breathtaking mountain heights.

It is not sensible to place our trust in any appeal that does not concretely and courageously respond to the actuality and responsibility of suffering (past, present, and future) in our world. It may be a sign of ethical sensitivity or, possibly, more dubiously, a manifestation of political cynicism (to offset the impact of Ronald Reagan's much criticized visit to the Nazi cemetery at Bitburg) for subsequent American leaders to visit the killing fields of the Holocaust. George Bush while President in 1987 did visit Birkenau, perceptively writing in the visitors' book: "In remembrance lies redemption." Whether this latter visit was sincere or calculated, or some mixture, we may never know. But, more searchingly, remembering the atrocities of others, even if a genuine sign of empathy and solidarity, is not in itself redemptive if the human wrongs committed by the self remain unacknowledged.

To visit the survivors of Hiroshima suffering from radioactive disease might be redemptive for American politicians *if* the occasion of the first atomic attack on a human settlement was then and there acknowledged with remorse and without such lame rationalizations as were officially relied upon. In fact, American political figures have almost all stayed away from Hiroshima, probably not daring to look back, not being willing to dedicate themselves to the pursuit of a nuclear-free world, or not even being willing to confront the human consequences of an atomic attack. Such an unwillingness was underscored a few years ago by the furor caused by the prospect of a Smithsonian Institution exhibit of the damage done by the atomic attacks. The backlash was then so strong, despite five intervening decades, that the exhibit was dramatically scaled back so as to avoid all issues of possible American wartime criminality and ethical responsibility. We, as Americans, cannot yet look back on this human catastrophe in a humanly empathetic manner, and, paraphrasing Bush's comment at Birkenau, "without remembrance there is no redemption."

The path from a religious renewal to a political renewal is complicated, controverted, and still quite difficult to discern. As I have suggested, several assured features are present: (1) an ecological feeling for the wholeness of experience as primary; (2) a decentering of anthropocentric presuppositions about the divine plan and the locus of the sacred; (3) a grounding of religious and political life in the challenge of suffering, not only of humans, but of other animals and even the rest of nature as well; (4) a conviction that the creative and imaginative locus of energies is passing from those who currently preside over established hierarchies of state and church; (5) a revisioning of gender relations; (6) a trust in the cooperative potential implicit in human nature, as well as a distrust in a variety of "realisms" and "rationalisms" that claim human nature to be ineradicably aggressive and entrapped within current behavioral and organizational enclosures of relations of power and wealth; (7) a disenchantment with violence and intimidation as the means to achieve security, justice, revolution, and transformation; and (8) a pervasive pedagogy of tolerance as the foundation of citizenship, nationally and globally.

Among the controversies are those about whether to connect the politics of postmodern thought with left or progressive modernist causes—to have associations with established political parties, with organized labor, and with the extension of rights in relation to current structures of governance. Is the postmodern a continuation in a different direction or a new start?[13] A specific cluster of disputes concerns the degree to which the postmodern environmental ethos accepts the outlook of the egalitarian "deep ecologists," those who would altogether withdraw any privileged status from human strivings and aspirations, sharing resources on the basis of some sort of parity with animals, plants, and even rocks and mountains. Some of these radical adherents fall into the trap of encouraging an exquisite sensitivity to the feelings of the nonhuman and even inanimate world while turning away from the correctable torments of human society. But most postmodernists do not go nearly this far as they recoil from modernist alienation from nature.

Neither religion nor politics has, as yet, crystallized around a definitive embodiment of the postmodern. Fascinating explorations are, to be sure, being undertaken in response to particular felt urgencies of time and space. The varied experience of Green Party movements in various countries has revealed the tensions between the emergent postmodern and the waning, yet still formidable, modern.[14]

The inner tensions of Green politics represent different ways of deconstructing the modern at a given historical moment and in a particular place as well as conflicts between reformers seeking marginal change and radicals seeking fundamental transformation. There are closely related instances of grassroots activism in Asia, especially India, the Philippines, and Indonesia, which are intent in a Third World circumstance on revitalizing democracy by reversing the flow of energy from periphery to center and by stressing the primacy of the local and concrete.[15] In a more explicitly postmodernist religious frame are the base communities throughout Latin America, especially Brazil, which were initially the seedlings of liberation theology but persist more recently as exploratory frameworks for testing and evolving new styles and formats for politics.[16]

Similarly, the new social movements associated with feminism, peace, and the environment that have ebbed and flowed since the 1960s—with their distinctly transnational reach—are better understood as a quest for comprehensive renewal and societal transformation associated with the emergence of global civil society than as specific issues and programs.[17] In contrast, those societal, initiative-seeking, specific policy associations, such as International Physicians for Social Responsibility and Amnesty International (both validated by the receipt of Nobel Peace Prizes), are quintessentially modernist, seeking to nudge existing institutional frameworks into minimal decency without posing the slightest transformative threat.

The postmodern can be identified by its necessarily challenging character. The otherness it seeks can be grasped by a crude contrast with the modern: The postmodern reveres nature and reinterprets the human relationship to the cosmos, finding sacred and mysterious energy embedded in all forms of life.[18] From this embeddedness a new religious culture is beginning to be discernible, but its distinct contours and even its credo are still in the process of formation. Only glimpses appear on still distant horizons. As William Butler Yeats prophetically warns in his poem "The Second Coming," there are enough disturbing signs to put Bethlehem once again on alert!

Postmodern Religious Revisioning

The argument of this chapter can be summarized as follows.[19] The secularism of modernist civilization does not inspire confidence in its capacity to respond to fundamental challenges in the contemporary world: nuclearism, ecological decay, mass misery, and impending biotechnical breakthroughs. Indeed, these challenges are severe as a consequence of the modernist experience with technology, war, and indifference to nature. As a result of this situation, modernism is losing its hold over the cultural imagination. In reaction, a dynamic of cross-penetration is underway between politics and religion and among civilizations, producing a series of developments that can be either constructive (liberationist) or destructive (extremist). Politics is being reinfused with religious symbols and claims, whereas religion is being summoned to the trenches of popular struggle, including being enlisted in armed campaigns against this or that established order.

This breakdown of the modernist separation and antagonism between politics and religion represents a series of societal efforts to handle a new agenda of human demands. Perhaps most unexpected in this regard were instances of reconciliation in the latter stages of the Cold War between Marxism and Christianity in several Third World settings, a process that was one of mutual enrichment without any apparent effort to subordinate one to the other. This process was extremely threatening to established hierarchies, although with the ending of the Cold War, there is far less interest in and anxiety about ideological orientations associated with the Marxist heritage. Rome's defense of clerical privilege and its insistence on retaining fully centralized ecclesiastical control over matters of ritual and creed represented another kind of limiting response. Also, the United States government, with its persisting ideological fervor against socialist tendencies in the Third World, has refused to recognize this potential for reconciliation and continues to attack left governments that are religiously conditioned on the premise of their godlessness. Such a posture was again prevalent during the official visit of Pope John Paul to Castro's Cuba a few years ago. A modernist secular state may be far less religious than a state that is governed by a revolutionary movement influenced by the new Christianity of base communities and progressive religious outlook.

These concerns, at the core of current world conflict and ideology, remain entrapped within the essentially modernist framework relied upon in the conduct of international relations: distinct territorial states looking forward to an expansion of their productive capacities to promote economic growth as the most effective way by which to relieve the misery of their peoples. To find more effective and humane means to mobilize peoples to pursue these ends is a challenging, hopeful development, the full potential of which remains untested.

At the same time, there is emerging a postmodern political sensibility that is animated by an entirely different worldview. It, too, is a kind of religious politics or political religion, though it does not grow out of the hitherto dominant interpretation of established world religions, especially those of a monotheistic character in which the divine reality has been imagined to be above and external to nature or in which theology is rooted in ecclesiastical and patriarchal structure. The postmodern orientation is ecological and antipatriarchal at its foundation, finding spiritual coherence in the processes of nature itself. Safeguarding the miracles of creation—including the habitat for human and animal life—against violence, destructiveness, and pollution becomes the most critical religious undertaking, especially given our growing realization that natural life-support systems are under severe and growing strain.

The human species has a special coevolutionary capacity and responsibility. Unlike other species, we are conscious of our roles in the world and bear the burdens of awareness for disrupting the ecological order to such a dangerous and unnecessary degree. As such, we can respond to the pain of the world by devoting our energies and resources to various forms of restorative action and creating the institutional forms and public understanding that are needed for such a dramatic reorientation of behavior. This "conversion" from secularism is underway in various largely privileged enclaves of human existence, but to an uneven degree, and virtually not at all if influence is assessed by reference to powerfully entrenched governmental and globalizing market structures associated with a persisting hypermodernist enterprise.

The premodern anticipates the postmodern, although historically it gave way to the modern and hypermodern. The postmodern draws on the distant past, but it cannot reproduce it, although it can relearn ancient wisdom and adapt this knowledge to current world conditions. The acute sense of jeopardy, complexity, and technological unfolding and the sheer density and interpenetration of peoples and cultures in the contemporary world provide an assurance that the postmodern will be a new way forward, not a repetition. To succeed, the postmodern unfolding needs to involve both political renovation (to deal adequately with resources, relations among societies, group identity, gender relations, and human and nonhuman needs and aspirations) and a religious reawakening (the release of spiritual energy associated with this readjustment of role and mission).[20] To what extent Green politics, new social movements, reemergent indigenous peoples, and small communities of faith and resistance are vehicles of this postmodern possibility remains to be seen. Assuredly, each of these tendencies is expressive of a reaction against modernist encroachment and a partial revelation of what a fused religious and political postmodern consciousness imagines an alternative, preferred world might be. Such imaginings are being given a preliminary concreteness in the form of many discrete explorations, and cumulatively give rise to the hypothesis of a "global civil society." There is a common thread: the sense that the whole and the part are united in reality, not alternatives, and that problem-solving and value-realization require both attentiveness to wholes (shared participation in species, life, planet) and greater fulfillment for distinct parts (ethnic, gender, cultural specificities).[21] Nothing, as yet, has gelled into a pattern that can claim for itself the definitive *imprimatur* of postmodernism or that can monitor initiatives to decide whether or not their contribution is genuinely postmodern rather than merely antimodern.[22]

Globalization as a framework for comprehending the contemporary reality has given an added impetus to civilizational and religious identities.[23] Such a pattern reflects widespread concerns that a globalizing Information Age is inevitably a vehicle for a homogenizing Westernized world under the geopolitical leadership of the United States. Religion and cultural traditions are being both vitalized and threatened by such a project.

5.

Politically Engaged Spirituality in an Emerging Global Civil Society

Recent developments have made problematic the very character of politics, conceived of in relation to the control of power, which is best understood as the capacity to exert influence and exercise authority. The deeper challenges posed by violence against our habitat and against ourselves seem incapable of generating a reassuring political response. The main expressions of political life, such as elections, political parties, and even government itself, seem preoccupied with trivial short-term concerns and geopolitical projects and seem unwilling and unable to direct attention toward the fundamental challenges of the age. The foremost French cultural critic Jean Baudrillard writes dismissively that a "critique of the political is no longer worth the effort today. Let's move on, let's see what happens elsewhere."[1]

This chapter also reflects disillusionment with the conventional domain of politics. It reverses the political optic by claiming that transformative patterns of behavior will result from "spiritual" interventions in societal processes rather than from "mechanical" or "material" causes, or even, in some Hegelian sense, from the impact of historically appropriate ideas. These latter factors are, of course, influential, but not decisive when, as here, the primary concern is with transformation, a radical turning of consciousness, which depends on spreading and deepening the realization that human behavior in all its aspects needs to become far more respectful of the sacredness of life. Working to comprehend the concrete implications of such a transformation is the essence of politically engaged spirituality.

The most basic claim of this position can be understood by reference to sustainability. The old ways are not sustainable, either in the physical sense of survival or in the moral sense of tolerability.

We cannot and will not go on as before. Either our world will drift toward catastrophe or transforming mutations will occur, and, without adopting an apocalyptic tone, the time horizon for transformation seems to move closer, certainly no more than a matter of decades. Such an observation seems justified despite the end of the Cold War and the willingness of those prime monitors of the apocalyptic horizon—the editors of the *Bulletin of the Atomic Scientists*—to move the hands of their famed clock back a few minutes from the midnight witching hour. The dangers of nuclearism persist in various forms, and new aligned threats of biowar have entered the apocalyptic imagination, but the most disturbing menaces to the human species lie just beyond the latest frontiers of technological innovation, in the possibility of a genetically engineered "human" species of robot armies of "spiritual machines."

In the West, the modern age is drawing to an end, that is, the confidence that science and instrumental reason would ensure the progress of human society, the idea that religion and spirituality were essentially superfluous, and the hope that such secular ideas as political boundaries, sovereignty, territorial supremacy, and the rule of law would provide solid grounds for optimism about human destiny. Increasingly, none of these elements holds firmly: Science has approached dangerous limits by way of nuclear weaponry, biogenetics, and robotics; the secular path seems blocked by anxiety about ecological viability, and the organizing political concepts based on territorial fragmentation of modernity seem more and more anachronistic in the face of globalizing tendencies in domains of communications, information, and capital.

Although under siege, much that is modern continues to provide the dominant structure of our world situation. Yet at the margins there are encouraging signs of displacement, of new patterns and paradigms reshaping behavior and perception. To simplify, there are two varieties of postmodernism that while distinct are also linked. There is, first of all, critical postmodernism, the realization that the secular, technologically driven dynamic of consumerism and global markets is no longer, if it ever was, capable of producing either human happiness or any promise of a bright future, that we are increasingly menaced by the dangers of modernist implosion, and that the most that can be done within the modern framework is to resist the lure of false hope that is achieved by fastening onto some kind of coherent grand narrative that seems to offer us a new universal solution. Critical postmodernism has definitely helped us grasp the extent to which the world of socially constructed meanings is one that has, in Michel Foucault's phrase, been molded by the "discipline of power," but such knowledge tends to leave us stranded on this island of critical insight, producing over time a disabling sense of despair and futility.

But there is another set of possibilities, here labeled "reconstructive postmodernism." Such an orientation does not repudiate the achievements of the modern world but acknowledges their radical insufficiency in relation to contemporary challenges.[2] The reconstructive path is deeply influenced by an awareness of ecological limits and thresholds and by the actual and potential role of social forces and democratizing energies as historical actors embedded in civil society. It also takes account of globalizing tendencies, both those that operate to consolidate on the basis of a unified administrative capacity and those that struggle on behalf of the peoples of the world to maintain a positive appreciation of difference and diversity, with identities shaped by a vision of what the future might be if all goes well.

I associate reconstructive postmodernism in its historical embodiment with the emergence of something coming into being that may be properly named a "global civil society," the ensemble of transnational efforts to achieve human solidarity on behalf of a tormented and endangered planet. This new society is made up of those movements, citizens' associations, and informal networks that are virtually oblivious to boundaries of sovereign states.[3] The name of "global civil society" is intended to be a political statement, a relocating of public sentiment and energy that doesn't fully exist until it is conceptually acknowledged. The commitment of individuals to strengthen and construct global civil society is also recreating our understanding of citizenship, redirecting loyalties from the primacy of space (the idea of loyalty to our state and flag) to the primacy of time (loyalty to a future normative order that engages our reconstructive energies). Of course, the space identified here as global civil society is available and used for a variety of political undertakings, including those of regressive character. This chapter proceeds from these starting points, exploring in particular the central relevance of what is called here "politically engaged spirituality."

Specifying politically engaged spirituality is bound to be controversial, relying on interpretations that rest on faith (beliefs that cannot be demonstrated in a manner susceptible to scientific verification) in a global social setting that lacks civilizational unity, in the form of a shared mythic order, and even agreement on the nature of knowledge. There is a certain qualified, reluctant degree of consensus associated with an emergent human rights culture, and an associated affirmation of constitutional democracy as the foundation of legitimate government. The reluctance stems, in part, from oppressive structures and practices operative in many countries as well as from suspicions surrounding Western sponsorship of such undertakings. This suspicion arises from colonial memories of cruelty and exploitation but also from postcolonial renewals of interventionary diplomacy under a variety of humanitarian banners.[4]

Until quite recently, the West cohered around the unifying mythic order of scientific rationality, allowing Nietzsche's cry that "God is dead" to resonate, even when formally denied, especially among governing political and economic elites. The West encouraged a view of history that insisted that its own path to ascendancy would soon be gratefully adopted by the non-West. Religion was maintained as a social facade for political life in the West except in that most modernist of all political faiths, Marxism-Leninism, a dogmatic and encompassing claim to comprehend and control reality, otherwise known as "scientific socialism." Oddly, the Lenin cult in the Soviet Union first extinguished organized religion but then, while hardly blinking, quickly reintroduced religious worship in its most primitive form, idolatry.

The capitalist West superficially succeeded in secularizing political life, yet its victories of reason and humanism have been precarious, always remaining vulnerable to the return of dark, irrational, and fundamentalist forces. The Nazi eruption of the irrational in a barbarous form expressed, among many other things, the dangerous incompleteness of the modernist project, as well as the falseness of its linear vision of history, which was supposed to carry human experience to ever higher levels of attainment. In addition, there is the notable failure to supplant religion by reason in mass consciousness and a related confusion about the nature and reality of spirituality.

Organized religion has been a vehicle for the spiritual in many settings, but to the extent bureaucratized and joined to secular authority, religious institutions can operate suppressively toward spirituality. To illustrate, when papal authority is used to silence the attempts of such notorious Church radicals as Leonardo Boff or Matthew Fox to endow Christian theology with postmodern relevance, religion shows its suppressive face, while when the Dalai Lama or Thich Nhat Hanh address the destiny of their respective countries (Tibet and Vietnam) from an outlook of nonviolent reconciliation, religion and spirituality become mutually reinforcing. The choice may also be one of temperament: Daniel and Philip Berrigan, both Catholic priests and brothers united in their commitment to radical and risky expressions of politically engaged spirituality, chose different milieus. Daniel remained within the Church as a spirit warrior while Philip left the Church, forming an activist, spiritual community called Jonah House that seeks to heed the legacy of Christ unmediated by ecclesiastical interpretations. From my vantage point both brothers made valid choices, sustaining their commitments while differing in idiom and battleground, and indeed their lifelong comradeship testifies powerfully to their own celebration of such diverse choices.

Gandhi's Contributions

Mahatma Gandhi's relationship to both the theory and practice of politically engaged spirituality is seminal for an understanding of the past, present, and future of the orientation.[5]

Gandhi's extraordinary achievement was to comprehend modernity in all of its forms yet resist its powerful lure. Gandhi was able to reconnect politics with religion in an amazing manner that worked secular miracles while setting the spiritual imagination on fire. This reconnection of politics with spirituality had several characteristics: (1) nonviolence as ethos; (2) militant encounter with oppression as means; (3) recovery and positive reevaluation of indigenous cultural tradition and rejection of modernity as a natural and inevitable stage of development that could alone ensure a positive fulfillment of social goals such as peace, love, and justice; and (4) dedication to improving the conditions of the most oppressed as the decisive test of political sincerity. Gandhi's role in India achieved a glorious world historical validation by way of the dramatic British colonial retreat and has served in many diverse settings ever since as an inspirational reminder that transforming "power" does not need to be linked with technological superiority and translated into destructive capabilities and violent actions. The purity and demonstrated practicality of Gandhi's thought and life provided the world with a vivid spiritual pedagogy, despite Gandhi's inability to bring religious peace to relations between Hindus and Moslems, despite the subsequent rejection of his main teachings by his successors, including Nehru, his principal protégé, and despite the extraordinary irony of his violent death at the hand of a "principled" assassin. Gandhi's warnings about falling into the abyss of modern solutions when confronting India's massive social problems were ignored by India's leaders after independence. India's postindependence evolution has mixed moral exceptionalism with a rather cynical geopolitical normalcy. India's neutralism and championship of nonalignment during the Cold War illustrates moral exceptionalism. India's internal and regional reliance on coercion to sustain control over secessionist minorities and peripheral peoples are expressions of geopolitical normalcy. Crossing the nuclear threshold, a possibility in 1974 and a deliberative action in 1998, was a decisive embrace of geopolitical logic combined with an expression of the linkage between nationalist sentiments and warmaking capabilities.

However, Gandhi should not be regarded, for better and worse, as a pure traditionalist. Gandhi celebrated industrial simplicity, but he repudiated untouchability. He exhibited a selective response to India's traditions and cultural practices, seeking to maintain the communitarian and ecologically impressive qualities of pre-industrial India while overcoming the cruelties of India's caste consciousness. What distinguishes Gandhi's quest is not its exemplary quality as politically engaged spirituality (there are several other notable twentieth century exemplars—Albert Luthuli, Martin Luther King, Vaclav Havel, Petra Kelly), but the comprehensiveness of Gandhi's vision and its courageous embodiment in an imaginative repertoire of practices[6] that reflected both his deep insight into traditional India and his ingenious understanding of the "power of the people." Many subsequent explorations engendered by Gandhism have occurred in various settings, including the efforts to establish a nonviolent presence in combat zones by such civil initiatives as Witness for Peace and Peace Brigades International and the effort in the southwestern United States of the Sanctuary Movement to protect "refugees" from deportation, especially to El Salvador, by providing "illegal" solace and sustenance in defiance of U.S. Governmental policy. Almost inevitably, such nonviolent postures involve encounters with oppressive structures and imply a commitment to civil disobedience and civil resistance. Such oppositional postures have gained a legal status as a result of the embodiment of the Nuremberg Principles in international law after World War II.[7] It is now the duty of all persons to act in defiance of state authority and enacted law if necessary to avoid complicity with official criminality, by way of fundamental violations of international law in the areas of either war and peace or human rights.[8] It is possible to confuse this Gandhian tradition with its deformed double, religiously motivated action that is guided by fundamentalist certitudes. The world is currently accursed with many varieties of religious fanaticism, claimants of absolute truth prepared to kill the infidel or simply the "other"; deploying violence on behalf of their special vision of blessedness. Moderation and respect for others as embodied in the Enlightenment side of modernity can make even the most narrowminded secularism a welcome relief if only to offer an escape from religious warfare, persecution, and dogma.

As well, the developmental side of modernity has enabled a greater proportion of the peoples of the world to overcome poverty and hardship and should not be lightly cast aside. Such productive success is now, in turn, rubbing up against a variety of ecological limits, but it would seem unwise to abandon the emancipatory potential of technological innovation rather than to achieve sustainability by making a series of ethical and environmental adjustments. That is, politically engaged spirituality needs to be grounded in the unfolding realities of the modern world, sensitive to the material needs of people and the concreteness of their suffering. It is important to engage in dialogue across cultural boundaries, acknowledging specific traditions and belief of time and place while becoming aware of the growing relevance of wider, even universal, horizons of context (region, civilizations, world, cosmos) and identity (gender, race, class, species). The unevenness of specific circumstances, economically and culturally, makes generalizations suspect even as the dynamics of global capital and communications symbolically link the planet in a single, integrated, homogenizing grid, typified by the omnipresence of McDonald's and CNN and reinforced to an extent by a growing range of regional arrangements.

Taking the Initiative

Politically engaged spirituality implies both the will and the capability to intervene nonviolently yet with behavioral consequences, in situations of conflict and oppression. Such interventions can be directed at very local circumstances or at conditions of a more general character. My concern here is to connect such action with that portion of the world historical scene that relates to the emergence of global civil society. Thus, the relevant field of action needs to be transnational in scope and global in significance, suggesting as well an identity bounded by solidarity with humanity as a whole, thereby transcending traditional fragmented identities based on nationality, race, religion, civilization, and class. Three examples will be relied upon to exhibit more clearly the action or interventionary sides of politically engaged spirituality.

The first example involves an initiative by six prominent former winners of the Nobel Peace Prize in Thailand, who sought the release of Ms. Aung San Suu Kyi, the Myanmar (formerly Burma) political leader who epitomizes politically engaged spirituality, combining a commitment to the democracy movement in her country with a strong inner discipline shaped by Buddhist practice and belief. She has been held under house arrest for fourteen years and is herself a recipient of the 1991 Nobel Peace Prize. The Nobel laureates who called for her release were Oscar Arias Sánchez, former president of Costa Rica; Archbishop Desmond Tutu of South Africa; Mairead Maguire and Betty Williams, the leaders of a peace campaign in Northern Ireland; the Dalai Lama; and Adolpho Esquival Pérez, an Argentinian human rights leader who had exposed death squad activities in the 1970s. In addition, calling for her release were representatives of Amnesty International and the American Friends Service Committee, who were organizational recipients of the same coveted prize. Three other Nobelists, Mikhail Gorbachev, Mother Teresa, and Rigoberta Menchu, sent messages of support. The group praised the courage of Aung San Suu Kyi, affirmed her continued following among the people of Myanmar, condemned by name the military junta ruling Myanmar, and proposed an arms embargo comparable to that imposed on Saddam Hussein's Iraq after its invasion of Kuwait. The group also set up meetings with exiles and sought, without success, to enter Myanmar and meet with supporters of the democracy movement. The military rulers of Myanmar condemned the event as an unwarranted interference in their internal affairs, and the Chinese government asked Thailand to deny a visa to the Dalai Lama.

This initiative has had the effect of bringing the plight of Aung San Suu Kyi and of the Myanmar people to world attention, thereby generating some pressure on both world public opinion and on the regime. The assumption here is that moral eminence is a form of soft power, and that the willingness of leaders of this stature to travel for such a purpose to Thailand is an indication of the exceptional concern attached to the particular oppressive circumstance. The fact that Aung San Suu Kyi was herself a recent winner of the Nobel Peace Prize established a special bond and added legitimacy to this expression of solidarity. The spiritual dimension of such a political act is in the implicit conviction that the aggregated voice of moral authority has a weight in human affairs. Whether the weight is sufficient to achieve its end is another matter. Such an initiative has increased awareness and, by so doing, has made more widely known the persistence of this confinement of an internationally acclaimed political leader who was herself an adherent of nonviolent democratic politics. It has also solidified Myanmar's status as a pariah state. This type of initiative, although possible only on exceptional occasions due to the difficulty of mobilizing religious leaders who are operating on a demanding routine schedule, is illustrative of the role of moral authority in shaping the outcome of political struggle. It is an alternative to violence and not less likely to attain its goals over time.

A second example is connected with the 1990s debate about restructuring the United Nations Security Council. It is more than fifty years since the United Nations was established, with permanent membership and veto rights vested in the five victorious powers of World War II. A vigorous diplomatic campaign was waged to expand the permanent membership of the Security Council to seven by adding Japan and Germany, qualifying them both as financial superpowers and important states. Another line of reform emphasized representativeness and the changed global setting of the postcolonial world. In this view, India, Brazil, and Nigeria should be added as permanent members, or at least should be at all times represented by at least one member endowed with veto rights. Such directions of proposed reform reflected the workings of the modern world, with its emphasis on state power as measured mainly by military and financial capability and secondarily by the extent of territory and size of population. In this regard it is emblematic of modernity that the present five permanent members were, until 1998, the five announced nuclear weapons states in the world![9]

The dynamics of reform foundered on an unwillingness of the U.N. membership to agree on a formula for the expansion of the Security Council. In essence, the countries of the north, emphasizing efficiency, control, and ability to contribute materially to the work of the United Nations, could not reach a compromise with the countries of the south, which stressed a demand for representativeness reflecting world geography and civilizational diversity. The organization entered the twenty-first century with the same essential Security Council that emerged from a colonialist world in 1945. The point here is not to stress organizational paralysis but to suggest the boundaries of mainstream debate about global reform as a basis for proposing an alternative mode of approaching the issue of legitimating the Security Council. This alternative expresses the viewpoint of politically engaged spirituality, bringing to bear fundamental ethical perspectives on the overall approach to global security policy.

A politically engaged spirituality could approach the issue of U.N. reform in the Security Council from several different angles. For instance, instead of military and financial power, emphasis could be placed on moral attainments and normative qualifications: the realization of human rights at home, of generosity and nonviolence in foreign policy, and of commitment to a sustainable and equitable system of world order for the future. Another approach would be to give permanent membership to a government drawn from the group of economically disadvantaged or environmentally ravaged states. Suppose a panel of former winners of the Nobel Prize were entrusted with the authority to designate a state with the best moral record in their judgment to serve as a permanent member of the Security Council for a term of up to five years. More ambitiously, such a panel could also be empowered to suspend voting rights of a permanent member if it used force "aggressively," if it violated human rights severely, or if it failed to make diligent efforts to eliminate stockpiles of weaponry of mass destruction. What would it take to institute such drastic, yet desirable, reforms of the United Nations along such lines? My answer would be, "nothing less than a spiritual revolution!" That is, a different manner of conceiving and administering power. But revolutions do not happen without struggle. Proposing such ideas, as moral hypotheticals, now discloses the gap that separates conventional wisdom on what can be done politically to strengthen the United Nations from the spiritually guided wisdom that builds a future global civil society on the basis of a Gandhian ethos as well on the establishment of global democracy.

The third example is drawn from the experience of the Gulf War. After Saddam Hussein attacked Kuwait on August 2, 1990, occupying and later annexing the country, a sense of inevitability developed in subsequent weeks as to the prospect of war. At the time, this inevitability seemed to center on the reluctance of the U.S. Government to give sanctions or diplomacy an adequate chance to achieve a reversal of the Kuwaiti loss of sovereignty. The United Nations Security Council, severely tested by Iraq's flagrant disregard of international law and the U.N. charter, struck a Faustian bargain with the United States. It would effectively resist Iraq's aggression by relying on the military power and diplomatic leadership of the United States, effectively suspending its own constitutional framework by delegating unrestricted authority to its most powerful member and relying on war as the means to resolve an international conflict.

As the pattern formed, the militarist assumptions struck me as being destructive and unlikely to produce beneficial results over time. It seemed, during the closing months of 1990, to be a Greek tragedy in the making. I watched helplessly, able to foresee the horrifying outcome of this clash of forces. Could such historical tendencies be redirected in more constructive directions? Where was the will to resist this onset of a major war?

During the Cold War a geopolitical equilibrium existed and would probably have precluded this drift toward the Gulf War. In this earlier setting of bipolarity, Iraq would probably never have acted against Western strategic interests without receiving the prior approval of Moscow, which almost certainly would not have been given. Had it acted, fears of a wider war and of recourse to weaponry of mass destruction would have altered the pattern of response, making a negotiated withdrawal by Iraq far more likely. Furthermore, the stalemate between the superpowers would certainly have prevented the United Nations from authorizing recourse to war.

Also evident was the failure of the traditional peace movement. Those intent on avoiding war were confused by the U.N. auspices, by the demonization of Saddam Hussein, and by the general discrediting of left politics as a result of the collapse of Communism and the surrounding events in Eastern Europe and elsewhere. Global peace forces lost their focus after the collapse of the Berlin Wall in late 1989. Many individuals and groups around the world organized on behalf of peace during the Gulf Crisis, often holding large demonstrations, but their efforts were sporadic and did not have a mobilizing effect. Criticisms of U.S. Government belligerency and the militarist approach to the crisis were largely ignored by the media and made little public impact.

It was in this setting that together with a close friend I conceived, far too late and without adequate contacts, of a project based on what might be called "spiritual intervention" or, possibly, "applied spirituality." We asked the question, "What if several of the great religious leaders of the world could be persuaded to locate themselves physically in the combat zone—in the path of the tanks, bombs, and missiles—and remained on the scene until the crisis was peacefully resolved, which would have had to include at the very least Iraqi withdrawal from Kuwait?" In some respects, this idea built upon the efforts of citizens who participated in Witness for Peace and took part in the Peace Brigades, which actually went to the Iraqi frontlines. In some respects these initiatives by ordinary people required greater courage than my proposal would have required precisely because it was so easy for the media and political leaders to ignore their presence or to dismiss these soldiers for peace as an unwarranted and naive intrusion. To test the plausibility of bringing religious leaders to the Gulf, I contacted many friends in the two weeks before the 15 January 1991 deadline that had been imposed by the United Nations on Iraq.[10] We made feverish efforts to establish direct contact with several of these religious notables, a proposal was drafted, and specific inquiries were made to find out whether the Dalai Lama, Pope John Paul II, Archbishop Desmond Tutu, the Mufti of Jerusalem, and Thich Nhat Hanh were receptive to such an initiative. The logistics were themselves quite overwhelming, and we were unable to obtain unimpeded access to these religious luminaries, although persons in their entourage seemed uniformly interested and, in several instances, were excited and enthusiastic. In retrospect, such an approach, to have any reasonable hope of success on such short notice, would have required either the active support of eminent persons at high levels of prominence (heads of state, the Secretary General of the United Nations, other religious leaders) or would have had to evolve slowly and collaboratively over a period of weeks or months rather than days. The crisis seemed out of control by the time the spiritual intervention was being urged upon busy religious leaders for their consideration.

But the impulse beneath this initiative was the belief in the potential capacity for effective and, perhaps, decisive spiritual intervention in history on behalf of peace and justice. Beneath this belief was the historical memory of Gandhi's exploits, especially the way his unconditional fasts had contributed to the collapse of British colonial rule in India. Also relevant in my thinking was the successful 1989 risings against East European regimes that had nonviolently challenged entrenched, oppressive power, although not from a primarily spiritual perspective in the core sense used here, and acted out of a commitment to nonviolence and an acceptance of the risk of vulnerability in the course of confronting state violence. I believed at the time of the Gulf crisis that if spiritual leaders of sufficient stature, visibility, and conviction had, in fact, located themselves in the war zone, it would have altered the nature of the crisis, making a nonviolent outcome far more likely, especially if they were prepared to remain in a position of physical vulnerability for however long would be required, that is, until the crisis was resolved. In this event, the war might likely have been avoided and the sovereign rights of Kuwait restored. Furthermore, the posing of such a challenge to leaders of states, although not without problems associated with modernist views about the separation of church and state, would have generated an important debate on the relationship of religion, spirituality, and politics.

Several tentative conclusions emerge: (1) Spiritual intervention to avoid collective violence in confrontations between states could weight the outcome of an international crisis in a nonviolent direction, especially in settings where the more powerful side militarily was claiming the mantle of moral and legal authority and was acting under a mandate of the United Nations. (2) The availability of this instrument is not at all ensured, even if the right approach had been used, as religious leaders seem generally reluctant to encroach upon traditional conceptions of political space (secularism prevails) and because such leaders would have to rearrange their own institutional priorities and make themselves available in extraordinary circumstances for controversial roles involving possible physical danger. (3) If peace had been preserved in the Gulf as a result of such a spiritual intervention it would have inspired many people throughout the world to take a far more sympathetic and serious view of the relevance of "religion" to the human condition, possibly prefiguring a more general reunion of religion with spirituality. It could have contributed both to the reawakening of a politically engaged religious consciousness and to a more spiritually sensitive politics.

It is instructive, if depressing, to note what did occur by way of religious input, on the U.S. side. Episcopal bishop William Browning, the White House pastor and church leader of high prestige, counseled President George Bush against war. As January 15, 1991, the date of the U.N. ultimatum directed at Iraq, approached,

Bush replaced Bishop Browning with the famous evangelist, Billy Graham, who readily endorsed the war with supportive fervor. In effect, religion was treated as a resource useful to the warmaking project organized by the state, and if a contrary religious voice was heard it was merely cast aside by the peremptory authority of the prince. With such a role, religion is supposed to play its part in the patriotic war machine of the modern state by literally blessing recourse to mass violence. It should also be appreciated that Saddam Hussein also made an ultra-opportunistic use of religion, "discovering" Islam as a means of mobilizing mass support for his coming war with the infidel West and of presenting himself, despite an extreme secular past that included the persecution and execution of leading Iraqi religious figures, as a truly legitimate guide for society because a devout adherent of the Prophet. It is quite unnerving that these two men of little spirituality should have both invoked religious authority to validate their embrace of war.

The specific circumstances suggest a broader format. If organized religion is to achieve spiritual authority, it must respond independently to state power, unwavering in its commitments to peacefulness and justice as well as dedicated to the pursuit of spiritual goals in public as well as private space.[11] These spiritual goals need to accord with widely endorsed ethical goals such as the avoidance of war, the mitigation of poverty, struggles against oppression, and campaigns to restore and maintain nature and safeguard the sanctity of life. Only by being so engaged can religion in its main institutional forms respond to the spiritual needs of most women and men in our time. The validity and strength of this conviction, as well as its problematic character in light of opposition organized at the heights of most existing religious establishments, can be glimpsed in relation to the rise and fall of "liberation theology" in the Third World, its extraordinary mobilizing effects at the grassroots in poor countries but its susceptibility to cooption and institutional backlash. The bloody story of the efforts by even the hierarchy of the Catholic Church in El Salvador to stand with the poor against a merciless state is illustrative, as is the martyrdom of the Archbishop Oscar Romero who was assassinated as a reaction to his show of solidarity with the poor of the country, a casualty of a historic effort to reendow Catholicism with a core spiritual identity. Two kinds of backlash result within religious institutions in response to such efforts at renewal: a reactionary reflex by church authorities to discipline their own ministers who manifest politically engaged spirituality and a deliberate encouragement of evangelical and fundamentalist religion by political and economic elites as part of their wider project to restore stability to an unjust social order. Religious leaders have often been aligned closely with the upper echelons of economic and political interest groups in unjust social and political projects of domination. The struggles of the poor and disadvantaged or the extension of spiritual priorities onto the playing fields of secular authorities have been attempted throughout history, but generally only at the margins of organized religion. For these reasons, those with a spiritual orientation toward reality have often found churches, temples, and mosques to be "sterile" and "cold" and have devised for themselves or borrowed from elsewhere new nurturing formats for spiritual practices, some meditative, others activist. But these efforts to reconstitute a spiritual dimension have been successfully subordinated by most variants of organized religion, being tolerated or indulged to slight extents at the two social extremes: the very poor acting out of desperation and the very rich acting with the benefits of privilege, including status and resources.

A Reconstructive Moment?

A pervasive contingency undermines the knowledge claims of the modern project and revalidates competing claims deriving from art and religion. Indeed, the possibility of a reunion of science, art, and religion is the essence of a reconstructive postmodern project that is intended both to supplant modernism and to provide an alternative reading of present and future to that of deconstructive postmodernism.[12]

Spiritually engaged politics, embedded in historical circumstances, will not escape maelstroms of negative energy (or entropy) unless it both bonds with the created order of life and takes seriously human suffering in the world. Two further orienting ideas follow: Since our knowledge never rests on the hard rock of certainty, pessimism and optimism are equally misleading as interpretations of human destiny;[13] small acts of no apparent consequence are capable of catalyzing enormously significant changes, thereby making passivity and nonaction highly irresponsible. We can never be confident that our small acts will not have major effects, and thus to withdraw is never cognitively or morally justified. Given the limits of our mind in grasping reality objectively, we are dependent upon beliefs, values, vision, and interpretative perspective to guide our thought and action. Finally, experience and postmodern critiques of dualism help us understand that all boundaries are provisional and transgressable, making the other and the self a unity as well as a pair of distinct entities and making the personal and the political intertwined as well as separated.[14]

Conceiving of politics from these perspectives has many possible implications in concrete circumstances. A few of these will be considered in relation to our engagement with the future. One of the leading modern ideas has been associated with citizenship, specifically the special status conferred on an individual in society to enjoy the full range of rights and duties associated with membership in a political community. The citizen is traditionally situated in space delimited by reference to the territorial boundaries of a sovereign state and is expected to be loyal in relation to the government of that state, paying taxes and being willing to defend the state against its enemies from without, even with death, if necessary.[15] Such a conception of political identity is bound up with nationalism and a related politics of allegiance, which are undoubtedly the most abiding of all modern passions. However, such an appropriation of political identity does not work spontaneously when individuals are caught in states that encroach upon their ethnic identity; as the state exerts coercive power within its boundaries, it can often suppress or contain dissident identities, at least temporarily. At the same time, it cannot gain genuine allegiance from those who regard the state as associated with a rival nationalism.

We are now witnessing in many circumstances around the world eruptions of ethnic politics of the most intense sort, which often seek to restructure boundaries of states to correspond with the political aspirations of a particular set of nationalist claims. Such a process, however terrifying in specific instances, generally reflects democratizing pressures associated with exercising the right to self-determination. The extent of this "right" is a matter of controversy, reflecting both the fluidity of the legal doctrine and expansive patterns of diplomacy. The old consensus, held during the entirety of the Cold War, supported the view that self-determination was applicable as a repudiation of colonial rule but could never be validly exercised if an existing sovereign state was dismembered in the process. The right of self-determination as set forth in U.N. declarations and the two human rights Covenants did not correspond with such a restrictive reading, and the geopolitical climate of the 1990s turned out to be quite receptive to secessionist claims in a variety of settings.[16] Such political violence is, in a sense, an expression of the exclusivist character of the modern political sensibility. That is, it draws decisive distinctions between a collective self and a collective other, the former regarded as positive, the latter as negative, and treats the outcome of conflict as a matter of life and death for which no compromise is feasible and no exertion too great. The breakdown of order in much of sub-Saharan Africa and in the former Yugoslavia during the 1990s has given rise to the bloodiest of interethnic battlegrounds.

But the particular dynamic of discord in what had been Yugoslavia also reflects the ambitions of outside forces. Germany and Austria have been historically aligned with Croatian forces, while France and Great Britain seem primarily concerned with preventing German expansion in Europe and seeking to exert a Balkan influence of their own. Arms flow illicitly to the contending nationalities, media reports are distorted by insufficient information and ethnic partisanship, and global action was belatedly mobilized in various directions in response to chilling accounts of mainly Serbian atrocities. Often efforts of this sort express ulterior geopolitical motives, however justified on humanitarian grounds. However one conceives of these complex issues, the framework is modern, primarily concerned with territorial boundaries and loyalties and with the framing of political life by reference to clear limits. These limits rest upon the presumed lethal distinctions between "them" and "us," distinctions given a horrifying resonance recently in Bosnia and Kosovo by the phrase and resultant practices of "ethnic cleansing" that, in effect, carry the fracturing of humanity to its genocidal outer limit.

Reconstructive postmodernism shifts the locus of identity from the particular to the universal, but without dissolving the connective tissue.[17] Its guiding premise is unity, but as conceived on the basis of difference, especially by those who lack power and wealth. Unity *imposed* from without tends to be reductive, resting on the logos of Disney World and franchise capitalism, or coercive, reflecting paramilitary technique and military superiority. The cumulative result is a type of globalization from above, the outcome of current technological and administrative possibilities to organize the planet as a whole. Market forces of trade, investment, and finance are mainly working to achieve a borderless world guided and shaped by criteria of capital efficiency and military dominance. Such globalization marginalizes those who are unable to contribute within such a framework, creating vast and widening gaps between rich and poor within existing states and among states, roughly designated in north/south terms, although with important variations. No sense of global community emerges despite globalization, specific political aspirations being subordinated to the impersonal play of the market and further distorted by a variety of improper manipulations. Citizenship in such a world is definitely confused and weakened. It tends to be diluted in sentiment and attachment and to produce alienated attitudes based on indifference and professionalism, that is, based on a willingness to protect the interests of one's own state as a professional or military undertaking and not, as traditionally, on the basis of loyalty and affection.

The Gulf War of 1991 exhibited both modernist and postmodernist features. The commitment to resist Iraq's aggression was motivated by interests in oil but justified by the sanctity of territorial boundaries and the prohibition on recourse to force, concerns validated by the U.N. Security Council. The war was conducted as if Iraqi lives were of little account and American lives were of almost absolute value, an idea that, in the latter stages of the war, carried the distinction between self and other dangerously close to criminality.[18] At the same time, devastating Iraq was cynically combined with allowing Saddam Hussein, a brutal tyrant, to retain political control, partly because it was convenient for outside forces, especially the U.S. Government, to shift their regional attention from the menace posed earlier by Iraq to a potentially expansionist Iran. In the background was a U.S.-led coalition of anti-Iraq countries financed by centers of capital in Tokyo and Bonn, as well as by the Gulf oil producers. The United States, as a major military actor, turned a temporary profit of some $8 billion from the military operations, although the figure could be raised or lowered depending on how costs were calculated and how the cost of military operations were evaluated since the 1991 ceasefire. The main point here is to understand the Gulf War as an expression of a globalized economic order mobilizing its will and destructive capabilities to discipline and punish a dissident territorial challenger, a pattern that also correlates with the reimposition of northern control over a resource-rich region in the south, with the resolve by the Christian West to renew its crusader approach to relations with the more assertive side of the Islamic East and with the overall impact of the religious resurgence. Such is the complex nature of the latest geopolitical games.

But there were also postmodern aspects of the Gulf War.[19] First of all, the media coverage filtered by way of CNN disseminated a single set of heavily censored images to the entire world. Second, these images conveyed a war that resembled an electronic video game and did not portray the death and dying that resulted in a sense of war as hell. Rather, the destructive reality was anaesthetized, as when a pilot was quoted as saying of the initial bombing, "Baghdad was lit up like a Christmas tree." Third, the burning of Kuwaiti oil wells and the spilling of oil into the Gulf brought into focus the new relevance of environmental concerns, both as a desperate weapon of resistance on Iraq's part and as a dimension of conflict.

There are other ways to handle the breakdown of territorial order in the face of globalizing influences (including those associated with environmental concerns, the spread of AIDS, and the sweep of popular culture). One idealistic way is to make a spatial adjustment outward, declaring oneself to be a "citizen of the world." Allegiance is owed to humanity as a whole and not to a particular state with its biases and interests. We must ask quickly what is the institutional embodiment of humanity? Is it the United Nations that summons new loyalty? Such a transfer of sentiment, while understandable given the shared destiny of the species, seems confused and suspect. In the absence of a global polity it may be naive to associate citizenship with the world as a whole. The claim to be a global citizen is often confused because most dimensions of life are still controlled at the region, state, and substate level, and loyalties mainly regroup around these immediacies rather than move to more encompassing identifications. Global citizenship is suspect because whatever institutional presences of a global character now exist are themselves dominated by states, and especially by leading states. Although capable of constructive initiatives, the United Nations is better conceived as an instrument of geopolitics (the U.N. Security Council) and market forces (the IMF, the World Bank) than as the chrysalis of a global community. At best, the United Nations is a site of struggle, enabling more visionary perspectives to be globally manifest, especially during so-called "counterconferences" (for instance, at the U.N. global conferences of the early 1990s). These more spontaneous gatherings defy the sweet reasonableness of the official and formal, and often sterile, intergovernmental sessions.

The extension of citizenship beyond its territorial point of origin is a challenge to be fulfilled predominantly in *time*, not to be realized currently in *space*. Loyalties and energies can then be directed toward constructing a future that will safeguard and celebrate the created order and will engage in the struggle to eliminate those forms of suffering brought about by deforming social, economic, political, and cultural practices and structures. No satisfactory terminology now illuminates this redirection of emphasis. I have proposed the phrase "citizen pilgrim," which draws upon the religious sense of a pilgrim wandering the earth in search of a better country, what St. Paul in the Letter to the Hebrews calls a "heavenly country." My sense is this: We need to engage in the struggle both to resist the globalizing erasure of difference being promoted by market forces and to strengthen the globalizing ethos of solidarity that animates transnational social forces devoted to democracy and human rights. Whether by way of environmentalism, feminism, or cosmopolitan democracy, there is emerging a series of transnational social forces that do not rely on military weapons, monetary wealth, or elite status, yet is seeking to construct a global community on the basis of visions of justice and the values of human dignity.[20] These transnational social forces, animated by normative ends and still at an early stage of self-realization, are in the process of constructing a "global civil society."[21]

In my understanding of the historical situation there is a creative tension between these two sets of tendencies, globalization from above (market, states, institutions, the momentum of technocapital) and globalization from below (social movements, citizens' associations, informal networks, the momentum of normative and spiritual energies). Globalization from above is the latest phase of modernist consciousness, relying on technology and economic growth to contribute to global wellbeing, which is conceived mainly by reference to materialist and elitist interpretations of human fulfillment. Globalization from below is an exploratory phase of reconstructive postmodernism, stressing popular initiative, ethical concerns, and spiritual interpretations of human destiny. Such a schematic presentation is itself deceptively dualistic. In actual circumstances, these distinctions break down. Some initiatives by governments can have positive transformative effects, as most spectacularly illustrated by Soviet governmental behavior during the Gorbachev years or by the contributions to peace and justice on the part of the Vatican during the papacy of John XXIII. Contrary to this, civil society can unleash destructive forces that include lending wide support to exceedingly violent forms of ultranationalism (as in Yugoslavia) and religious extremism (as in India, several countries in the Middle East and North Africa, as well as in the United States). But the larger generalization still holds: By and large, governments, corporations, and international institutions are seeking to create the conditions for extending their high-tech civilization on a planetary scale with no serious questions asked about human and ecological consequences, while grassroots normative initiatives are mainly moved by a dedication to the wellbeing of the created order and by a commitment to engender postmaterialist possibilities for social and economic life, thereby establishing a nexus for spiritually engaged politics.

Any societal order is partly behavioral, partly mythic. A societal order never has a tangible embodiment as a totality in time and space but is an attribution of reality that summarizes convergent activities and provides an affirmation of a coherent set of attitudes, beliefs, and relationships. To posit the existence of global civil society is thus a political act, a description of what is, an interpretation of what is emerging, as well as a desire for what is not yet. The thickening of transnationalism in many forms constitutes the empirical foundation of an emergent global civil society. To identify this trend with the emergence of a global civil society is intended, as well, to provide a kind of fictive home country for citizen pilgrims and to offer adherents to cosmopolitan democracy a social reality additional to those associated with market and statist forces. As global civil society lacks independent sources of wealth and does not rely on military capabilities yet is the scene of intense political struggles for survival (indigenous peoples, environmental agenda) and for dignity (human rights), a new set of orientations toward politics is taking shape, and it is with these orientations that we rest our main hope for the future of spiritually engaged politics, both the ethos and practice of nonviolence, the compassionate identification with those most victimized by present conditions, and the core preoccupation with ecological balance. In the end, reconstructive postmodernism presupposes spiritually engaged politics, not in some prepackaged, theologically evolved form, but as manifest in the myriad variations on the central theme, itself expressive of the diversities in the world and of the unevenness of perception, cultural standpoint, aspiration, historical occasion, and material circumstances.

Perhaps the awakening that politically engaged spirituality entails rests in the end on compassion directed toward suffering, waste, and shortsightedness, a reflex of the spirit in response to the seen and felt indecencies in the world as now organized, or, to quote from a poem by Adrienne Rich:

> The light of outrage is the light of history
> Springing upon us when we're least prepared[22]

6.

Hans Küng's Crusade: Framing a Global Ethic

For the last decade the celebrated German theologian Hans Küng has devoted much of his formidable intellectual and political energy to promoting a "global ethic" as the key to peace and a sense of a shared human community in an increasingly globalized world. The campaign has been successful, if measured in such conventional ways as contributing centrally to influential formulations on global policy by world religious and political leaders, engaging even the energies of the InterAction Council, a respected voluntary civic association whose members are former heads of state.

The project of a global ethic also directly and explicitly challenges Samuel Huntington's widely debated contention that world civilizations are on an unavoidable collision course. Küng, as might be expected from such a renowned theologian, also links the prospect of a global ethic to his conviction that a religious grounding for ethical claims encompassing the human species is at once indispensable and possible. Despite this, as would also be expected from Küng on the basis of his earlier work, he supports the adoption of a global ethic only if formulated in a manner that invites participation by nonbelievers and secular humanist perspectives as well as by adherents of non-Christian world religions. Küng strongly favors maximal inclusiveness in relation to the form and content of a proposed global ethic.

It is difficult to situate historically a project to establish the authority of a global ethic, given an intellectual terrain in which the mainstream political imagination seems currently preoccupied by the dialectical tension between globalization and fragmentation.[1] Against such a background, it is necessary to raise the awkward question as to whether Küng's call for a global ethic, articulated most fully in his *A Global Ethic for Global Politics and Global Economics*, is at all politically relevant within such an unfolding global setting.[2] I will set forth Küng's argument, as presented in *A Global Ethic*, situating it in contemporary world order thinking, and then evaluate its contribution to the ongoing debate about whether the sovereign state is being superseded and, if so, in what respects. In essence, the idea behind a "global ethic" is to launch a political project for human betterment that solicits the involvement of religious and political leaders throughout the world and subsequently establishes a climate that fosters improved intercivilizational communication and understanding.[3]

Such an assessment of this latest effort by Hans Küng should be read against a background of admiration for the integrity, courage, and wisdom that has characterized his long life as an engaged Christian theologian who has weathered the turbulent storms that swept across twentieth century Germany.[4]

While considering Küng's campaign for a global ethic, which seemingly is directed mainly at leadership circles within government, religious arenas, and in civil society, we need to keep in focus the complex question of whether ethical argument can ever provide sufficient *agency* for adaptive global change. Or, alternatively, whether such agency has become superfluous because integrative trends, often identified with "globalization," are by themselves pushing toward a unified world community for which a global ethic is likely to emerge spontaneously as a *consequence*. It may be helpful to analogize the evolution of a "global ethic" with that of a "national ethic," which is associated with the democratization of the modern sovereign state over a period of the past several centuries, including the struggle and eventual commitment to uphold the "rights" of citizens.[5]

Hans Küng's Argument for a Global Ethic

Starting Points

Küng starts from a concern that there is missing from influential political thought and from cultural space what he calls *"a realistic vision of the future."*[6] For Küng this is a serious, perhaps fatal, deficiency, as "problems continue to press in and the pressure is becoming greater, since today not only questions of national destiny but global questions, even that of the very survival of humankind, are on the political agenda, especially for Europeans and Americans."[7] There is an urgency about Küng's tone, clearly intensified by his sense of the then-approaching millennial threshold. At the same time, Küng wants to avoid a series of traps that he views as particularly tempting for someone of religious persuasion. More specifically, it is important for Küng to avoid the negative connotations of mere moralizing about a better future and of positing utopias that have no chance of being realized.

The promotion of a global ethic, in contrast, seeks to engage with power and the powerful and link their sense of national interest to the relevance of the "spiritual and cultural foundations of humankind."[8] In this respect, Küng seeks to avoid falling into either the trap of "political naivete," lecturing to those holding positions of political influence without an appreciation of the role of power in confronting evil challenges that arise in the world, or that of "moral arrogance," associated with a sense of unconditional self-righteousness. Küng respects those with responsibilities in the domain of power and seems genuinely aware of the fallibility of his own ethical intuitions, thereby insisting on subjecting his own ideas to continuous reflection and self-criticism.

Despite this nondogmatic and reflexive posture, Küng's analysis is not at all tentative. He describes himself as a "passionate advocate of reason and undeterred visionary," placing himself in the tradition of Immanuel Kant's *Perpetual Peace*. This strikes me as an accurate assessment, although it needs to be contextualized in the setting of the contemporary world, which emphasizes the many facets of globalization as well as the post–Cold War climate of secular nihilism and religious extremism. For Küng the central challenge is to mobilize the positive potentialities of religion, politics, and economics as normative counterweights to the destructive tendencies that are otherwise likely to engender a bloody era of "culture wars" and "religious wars."[9]

Giving the Devil His Due, and More

One of the most distinctive features of Küng's advocacy of a global ethic is its engagement with the worldview of political realism. The substantive argument of *A Global Ethic* is rooted in a rather detailed and generally sympathetic consideration of a realist orientation toward the behavior of states, taking a close look at the career and outlook of such exemplary realists as Cardinal Richelieu, Chancellor Metternich, Otto von Bismarck, and, most of all, Henry Kissinger. These were each individuals who were widely admired (and despised) for their capacity to manipulate the foreign policies of their countries in a manner that denied human solidarity and who conceived of the state as the only internationally relevant form of human community. Küng concludes that realism of this statist variety has provided "the *political paradigm of modernity*" (as contrasted with the Christian universalism of the medieval period), but that it is increasingly in a shadowland, being "caught up in a fundamental crisis which reveals the moral doubtfulness of all real politics."[10]

Küng relies on Kissinger's *Diplomacy* as the authoritative text of realism for the modern era, which in turn is treated as the currently dominant approach to world order.[11] Küng treats Kissinger's career as a diplomat with the greatest respect, calling him "a brilliant analyst of modern and contemporary politics."[12] Kissinger provides, then, the exemplary case of scholar/diplomat who, fairly conceived, illuminates the outlook of the realist, as well as the strengths and weaknesses of the position from the perspective of global policymaking. Like Metternich in the nineteenth century, Kissinger sought stability and security by way of a geopolitical power balance, and just as Metternich sought a new balance after the Napoleonic Wars, Kissinger sought to find a comparable balance in the midst of the Cold War. Küng credits Kissinger with various diplomatic achievements, perhaps most notably his role in opening the U.S./China relationship as part of his overall effort to exert maximum pressure on the Soviet bloc and create a favorable balance for the West.

While appreciative of realist skills, Küng is also sharply critical. He reads Kissinger as making "an eloquent and seductive *plea against* an American '*idealism*'" and "*a plea for a power politics oriented on European statesmen of the past.*"[13] As Küng notes, Kissinger is intent on repudiating what he sees, along with others, as a deficiency in the American approach to global politics, one that reached its climax during the latter stages of the presidency of Woodrow Wilson. Kissinger reserves his plaudits for Theodore Roosevelt, described admiringly as epitomizing the "warrior statesman," while scorning of the efforts of Wilson to construct a new and more just world order after World War I as the essentially misguided undertaking of a "priest-prophet."[14] Despite this historical dismissal, Wilson is taken seriously because Kissinger views variants of his idealism as dominant in America's approach to the world and responsible for recurrent American misassessments of national interests as realistically calculated.

As with Kissinger, Küng appears to view this tension in American political culture as genuine and significant. He sees in America a serious effort to find a way to participate in the world without abandoning morality and views this quest with approval and a sense of the persisting relevance of such an orientation. Thomas Jefferson's contention that states should adhere to the same moral standards as is expected of individuals in their dealings with one another is regarded as expressive of the most admirable facet of American political culture.

Küng also looks back critically at Kissinger's presentation of the high and low points in past statecraft and challenges his assessments. In particular he finds Kissinger's admiration for Richelieu badly misplaced, contending that not only the French nation and its people but Europe as a whole suffered from Richelieu's ruthless pursuit of French expansionism. Küng views these realist excesses as built into behavior that is neglectful of moral restraint. In this same spirit, he points to the eventual failure of the Nixon presidency, in which Kissinger served so prominently, as resulting from its moral bankruptcy.[15] Küng endorses the assessment of Kissinger's biographer, Walter Isaacson, that the victory of the West in the Cold War was not a vindication of realism as an approach to international relations. The West, according to Isaacson, won the cold war mainly because "the values offered by its system...eventually proved more attractive."[16] The burden of Küng's argument is that the realism claimed by the realists is often an illusion, that history moves more consistently in response to the value preferences of people, and that it is essential for a government to discover prudent means to combine its ethical constraints with its material interests.[17]

But Küng has additional adversaries to worry about. He seeks, in all respects, to avoid extreme positions, whatever their metaphysical claims. He opposes utopian movements that overlook the actualities of power and supports the need to oppose the forces of evil by warfare, if necessary. Küng acknowledges the importance of bringing to bear countervailing power in the context of addressing the menace of Hitler and Naziism, and he views Western resolve in the face of Soviet expansionist threats in a favorable light. Similarly, and possibly with a more special insight, Küng seeks to distinguish his advocacy sharply from that of religious fanaticism in any shape. The ethical absolutism of extremist religion tends to be exclusivist and inconsistent with the inclusiveness and spirit of mutual respect and solidarity associated with a global ethic. For Küng an indulgent secularism is equally unacceptable, reducing the meaning of life to a crude materialism that often takes the form of obsessive consumerism, a planetary cultural force under the dominion of the economic globalists.

As an ethical stance, Küng aligns his viewpoint with Aristotle's "golden mean," which is situated between the power-driven and "amoral realism" of Kissinger and one or another form of "ideological fanaticism," whether from right, left, or from extremist manifestations of organized religion.[18] In considering the rise of the sovereign state and its increasingly nationalist credo as a historical process in Europe, Küng questions the inevitability of Machiavellianism.[19] He selects Erasmus of Rotterdam as exemplary, a historical personality who traveled the middle path between the "medieval fanaticism of the Counter-Reformation" and the "cynicism of modern real politics."[20] On this middle path, the Aristotelean mean, Küng calls particular attention to the evolution of international law, referring to the Spanish school jurists Francisco Suarez and Francisco de Vitoria but specially regarding the contributions of Hugo Grotius, often called the founder of modern international law.[21] Tellingly, Küng observes that "none of these names appear in Kissinger's work" [on diplomacy] despite its length of over 1,000 pages.[22]

For Küng World War I was an "epoch-making global upheaval" that led to the dismantling of a Eurocentric world and the beginning of postmodernity, including the rise of "*a new paradigm of politics.*"[23] This process of transformation was later associated with the emergence of a more "polycentric" world that was also "post-colonial... and post-imperial."[24] Küng associates Woodrow Wilson with an ethically meaningful response to this set of circumstances. This association is based on the insistence that in the future global security would not be able to depend on balance of power adjustments but would require a collective security mechanism managed by the organized international community, an idea initially institutionalized by way of the League of Nations and carried forward into the present by the United Nations. Wilson also supported the idea of a "peace with justice" for affected peoples, based famously on the application of the principle of self-determination. It should be recalled that Wilson did not have an expansive view of self-determination. He was thinking only of the remnant peoples that had comprised the fallen Hapsburg and Ottoman Empires. He had no intention of encouraging the peoples living under European colonial rule to rise up in revolt and refrained from even urging their gradual emancipation.

Küng views Wilson ambivalently, as a counterpoint to Kissinger. Wilson is called a "hopeful-hopeless idealist"[25] who seemed unable to bring his vision of the future into the domain of effective politics, given the prevalence of a fairly cynical brand of realism among European leaders of the time. But in the end Küng seems disposed to believe in Wilson's approach, writing, "[t]he peace with justice of the 'idealists' would have been more realistic than the *dictated peace* of the realists; it would have spared the world a second, even more devastating, world war."[26] Such a retrospective account is not altogether convincing. After all, the drift toward Hitlerism and the renewal of major warfare was overdetermined, a confusing consequence of many interlinked factors, and cannot be convincingly reduced to the impact of any one cause. Having said that, there is no doubt that the harshness of the Versailles Peace Treaty was a major conditioning force, although it is not at all evident that a more diligent implementation of Wilson's conception of the peace would have worked out any better or differently for Europe and the world. Wilson's view of the role to be played by the League as an agency of war prevention did not correspond at all with the endorsement of sovereign rights of states or with the realist outlook of political leaders who continued to control policymaking and military capabilities. Arguably, Wilson did little more than offer a visionary template that could never have been actualized successfully in the world as politically organized at the time. The same dilemma has persisted in the U.N. era. The famous promise of the U.N. charter "to eliminate the scourge of war" is an instance of inspirational language, but the body of the Charter itself and, even more, the capabilities and experience of the organization, as well as the surrounding geopolitical milieu, have reaffirmed the primacy of Westphalian statecraft.[27]

Küng's overall view of developments after 1918 seems complex and inconclusive. For while he appears to endorse Wilson's approach, he takes critical note of the American withdrawal from Europe as well as repudiates the legalist futility of legalizing and moralizing gestures of the sort embodied in the Briand-Kellogg Pact of 1928, which purported to outlaw aggressive war. Küng is not impressed by such initiatives and believes that to alter warmaking it is necessary to back up a renunciation of war with "effective sanctions" that could be brought to bear upon a potential aggressor.[28]

Despite the rejection of Wilson's crusade for a "new world order," his undertaking does represent for Küng an irreversible welcome rupture in the history of international relations, which validates an argument that a postmodern paradigm was being engendered after World War I. For Küng, "[t]he art of politics in the postmodern paradigm consists in combining political calculation (or modern real politics) convincingly with ethical judgment (ideal politics)."[29] Küng insists that *"there will be no new world order without a new world ethic."*[30] He goes on to clarify the nature of this requirement, explaining that "the global ethic is a *basic consensus* on binding values, irrevocable criteria and basic attitudes which are affirmed *by all religions* despite dogmatic difference, and which can indeed also be contributed by [sic] *nonbelievers.*"[31]

On this basis, Küng seeks to identify a *"minimum ethical consensus"* which is deemed a possible and necessary project due to the emergence of certain global developments. He stresses "a community of destiny on our spaceship earth" and a TV-generated shared awareness of various struggles for "truth" and "justice" that build transnational bonds of solidarity.[32] Küng relies on Michael Walzer's notions of "moral minimalism" and a "'thin' morality" to help orient this search for ethical norms that are devoid of specific cultural and religious content.[33]

Where does this lead? On the basis of study and reflection, Küng suggests that the global ethic consists of two fundamental precepts that are embedded in each of the world religions:

- every human being must be treated humanely
- what you wish done to yourself, do to others; also formulated negatively, what you do not wish done to yourself, do not do to others[34]

These two normative ideas are then to be elaborated and sustained through reliance upon a series of directives that are embodied in all world religions, the commitment to: a *"culture of nonviolence and respect for all life," "a culture of solidarity and a just economic order," "a culture of tolerance and a life of truthfulness," "a culture of equal rights and partnership between men and women."*[35]

The bearing of religion on the global ethic is subtle yet vital. After all, at a superficial level the global ethic can be—and has been—affirmed in various arenas without any reference to religion. Consider, for instance, the plea for global values in the various writings of the World Order Models Project, in the final report of the Commission on Global Governance, in the Declaration on Human Responsibilities of the InterAction Council, and in the articulations of Parliamentarians for Global Action.[36] Küng himself suggests that the confirmation of the emergence of a global ethic can be best discerned by an alleged trend toward giving human rights a priority over the pursuit of economic self-interest.[37]

Küng is, of course, acutely conscious of the Enlightenment tendencies to marginalize the relevance of religion in public space. He rejects such marginalization: "Those who banish religion create a vacuum; at any rate they have to say what they have to offer in its place in this time of growing disorientation and pseudo-religiosity, particularly for many young people who are in search of meaning and orientation in values."[38] Instead of sidelining religion, it becomes important to appreciate "[t]he integrating function of religion which cannot in the end be replaced by any philosophy or even any ethic."[39] Küng believes that only religion has sufficient influence on a mass level to produce the sort of fundamental readjustment of focus on a behavioral level that is being proposed more abstractly as an implicit global ethic. In this sense, Küng conceives of the articulation of a global ethic to be essentially an intellectual task for the elite, whereas its implementation would be political and would depend on widespread public acceptance.

Küng lends concreteness to the claim of ethical relevance by discussing various concrete realities, including his view of the three main paths that an integrating Europe might follow. The first is what he calls "*Technocratic Europe*," the functionalist Europe of the Brussels' bureaucracy, essentially a materialist bargain for the sake of higher economic growth and bigger profits; it overlooks what is, for Küng, the central reality that "Europe needs *a spiritual and ethical renewal!*"[40] The second, somewhat surprising, path that Küng identifies is labeled "*the restoration of a Christian Europe*" and is depicted as a neo-Medieval project of the Catholic Church and its current pope, John Paul II, to re-Catholicize Europe along hierarchical, essentially antimodern and antidemocratic lines that are exclusivist in character. Küng regards such a project as deeply unacceptable on ethical grounds, as well as incompatible with the values and preferences of the overwhelming majority of Europeans, including those who regard themselves as Catholic. What is surprising, and revealing in its way, is why Küng finds this conception of a Christian Europe of sufficient relevance to be put forward as a plausible scenario for the future. It may not be remiss to suspect the influence of autobiographical factors! Only the well-known encounter between Küng and the Vatican could explain giving such weight to a scenario for Europe that is completely neglected by other analysts.

As might be anticipated, the preferred third path for Europe is identified as "*Europe with an ethical foundation*." This Europe would essentially give regional effect to the global ethic and take positive account of the plural, democratic developments on the continent, but would also seek to give a moral and spiritual dimension to the emergent European reality that overcomes the shadow sides of modernity. Küng, again not surprisingly, is dubious about the effects of extreme secularism, individualism, and pluralism that push modernity toward an atomizing, consumerist, and materialist future. In this setting, he finds that "patchwork religion" does not provide a sufficient sense of ethical and spiritual cohesion. In Küng's words, "secularization and rationality cannot so easily replace tradition, religion and mystery."[41] It is here, at this point, that Küng's distinctive vision comes to the fore. In contrast to the exclusivism attributed to the official Catholic approach, Küng favors an ethical Europe built on inclusivity and premised on a sense of responsibility toward others, an ethic that is at once "*liberating*" and "*binding*," and at the centerpiece of the efforts of churches and of organized religion generally.[42] This regional orientation should be outwardly inclusivist, as well, conceiving of relations with non-Europeans as falling within the same framework of tolerance and acceptance.

The indispensable role of religion is to give depth and cohesive power to an ethical perspective, which is not possible for a humanistic ethos of similar content. Here Küng offers his own witness as a nondogmatic, nonsectarian yet devout Christian. For Küng this participation in a distinct religious tradition gives a rootedness to solidarity with others as well as provides the sense of awe and sacredness that fully empowers individuals and groups to act for transcendent ends while situated in the lifeworld. Küng's position here is subtle and complex, as he strongly believes in the complementary relationship between religion and ethics, but he wants to keep open spaces for nonbelievers, who can qualify as participants in an ethical Europe.

Küng also extends these ideas to the phenomenon of globalization, seeking again to find common middle ground that accepts the basic momentum of late modernity but trying to modify it benevolently through the influence of a global ethic. The difference between the regional and the global is a matter of scope and degree, especially with respect to intercivilizational relations. Küng sees the future beset by the same twin dangers of reductive secularism and fundamentalist religion. Küng's middle path involves affirming religious identities of a traditional character but infused by a global ethic. Küng makes clear that he does not advocate some homogenized universal religion but rather seeks a religious revival built around the shared universalist elements of each major world religion. On a global level, Küng sees the need to address business leaders as well as politicians and is concerned about environmental decay and human rights as two vectors of accountability that market forces have not taken seriously enough in their relentless pursuit of profits and growth. Without a global ethic, Küng sees little hope for a sustainable and equitable global future, but he finds encouragement in the moves of world capitalism at Davos and elsewhere to depart from "market fundamentalism" and advocate "responsible globality."[43] There are many nuances of policy that give a rich texture to Küng's advocacy, but the essential message of bringing a global ethic to bear seems admirably simple in conception and application.

Secularist Alternatives to an Inclusive Global Ethic

To understand the particularity of Küng's perspective and that of kindred efforts that he has inspired and deeply influenced, such as the Parliament of the World's Religions and the Universal Declaration of Responsibilities of the InterAction Council, it seems helpful to consider briefly some alternative initiatives that proceed from similar normative motivations. Such a broadened inquiry highlights both differences and similarities, but also shows that the modern world of states is giving way to a still undefined "postmodern" world, one premised on a shared human destiny that calls for a global mode of assessment and prescription. The point being that modernity circumscribed the political imagination by reference to the territorial sovereign of the state, whereas postmodernity, while generally acknowledging the persisting importance of the state, is less clearly bounded and definitely more plural, ranging from civilization to region to world and, finally, to cosmos and universe.

Hans Jonas

A seminal figure in this resituating of normative horizons is Hans Jonas, a thinker who Küng acknowledges as leading the way. Jonas argues the case for a new sense of human responsibility, one that would respond primarily to the threats posed by dangerous technological innovations that manifest the "vulnerability of nature." Unlike Küng, Jonas rests his hope for response on a postreligious foundation as "the gods... are long gone."[44] Jonas is much more a child of the Enlightenment than Küng, conceiving of religion as essentially superseded by the rise of secular reason but believing that a benevolent future depends on grounding action in public spaces on an ethical view of human nature, which includes what he calls "lengthened foresight, that is, scientific futurology."[45] Jonas rejects the earlier optimism of the Enlightenment, with its perspective based on hope and the idea of progress, and instead calls for "an imaginative heuristic of fear" to avoid future disaster.[46]

Comparing these two figures, what is most notable, aside from their views as to the relevance of religion, is their differing ethical priority. Jonas emphasizes the need to expand the domain of reason so as to take account of dangerous future prospects before it is too late, thereby redefining the location of responsible collective human action. In contrast, Küng sees the problem of responsibility in more spatial terms by reference to the tensions between civilizations and belief systems and by the assaults on human identity being mounted by consumerism on one side and by fundamentalism on the other. Jonas worries that human survival is in jeopardy without bringing longer term considerations to bear, whereas Küng, although mindful of survival dimensions of the present reality, is primarily preoccupied with the ideological dangers posed by the drift toward an irresponsible globalism.

World Order Models Project (WOMP)

Ever since the late 1960s, WOMP has been engaged in a collaborative project among scholars from different parts of the world to promote a just and equitable world order based on the acceptance of cultural and ideological differences. However, these differences would be united by a shared commitment to a series of articulated world order values that are posited as universal. These values, while variable in specification, were abstractly formulated around four normative ideas: the minimization of political violence, the maximization of economic wellbeing, the promotion of social wellbeing and human rights, and the promotion of environmental sustainability. Such values were partly conceived as responses to serious shortcomings of the existing world order system: the war system, massive poverty and inequality, oppressive forms of governance, and environmental decay. WOMP encouraged the formulation of different recommendations for the future and was concerned with facilitating the reform of world order in an era of anticipated globalization.[47] By and large, the WOMP enterprise was ambivalent about the relevance of religion to the possibility of a better future, yet it shared with Küng a strong attachment to an agreed global framework of values.

Küng's approach, grounded in religious consciousness, stressed very fundamental ethical principles relating to right action, whereas WOMP's secular grounding led it to emphasize ethical ideas that were historically relevant as responses to salient problems of global scope. The two perspectives can be seen to be complementary, and there is an encouraging convergence. Küng has recently grounded his global ethic on an analysis of substantive challenges relating to the future of Europe, including an approach to ethnic conflict in the Balkans and to the regulation of the world economy. At the same time, WOMP appreciates increasingly the relevance of culture, which is shaped by religious traditions, and of the religious resurgence to mobilizing social forces committed to achieving "humane governance" at all levels of political authority, from the local community to the world.

Commission on Global Governance

This commission, composed of prominent individuals, many of whom have or have had distinguished careers in important government posts, issued a report in 1995 under the title *Our Global Neighborhood*. As this title suggests, the normative premise reflected integrative trends in the world that were giving increasing relevance to the metaphor of "neighborhood" both as description and proposal. Even more than WOMP, the Commission avoided any direct reliance on religious outlooks or terminology but shared with Küng the conviction that a global ethic was possible and necessary, and its members and staff were likely familiar with Küng's advocacy and quite possibly with the Declaration of the Parliament of the World's Religions. There is a definite similarity of outlook. The commission assumed the universality of the golden rule, urged the relevance of "religious teachings around the world," and invoked the U.N. Charter's emphasis on "inherent and inalienable rights of members of the human family."[48] Because of the absence of a metaphysical foundation, the Commission's advocacy is based on pragmatic and consequential reasoning rather than on intrinsic considerations. For instance, it encourages a shared global ethic by reasoning that "[o]ver the long run, rights can only be preserved if they are exercised responsibly and with due respect for the reciprocal rights of others."[49]

The Commission's emphasis was placed on widely shared "core values" (as supplemented by an emergent "global civic ethic of specific rights and responsibilities shared by all actors" and by an expanding body of international legal norms that were gradually altering claims based on sovereign rights and the principle of self-determination), including respect for life, liberty, justice and equity, mutual respect (tolerance), caring, and integrity (a counter to corruption).[50] The report is very sensitive to the importance of respecting differences that derive from various cultural backgrounds while at the same time encouraging dedication to the unified interests of humanity that transcend the fragmenting visions of nationalism, statism, and excessive marketization. It conceives of the imperatives of policy to be linked to the promotion of human rights, democracy, the United Nations, international law, humanitarian intervention, and the role of global civil society.

Although relating more closely to an immediate agenda of global reform than Küng did, the Commission on Global Governance is equally clear about the singular importance of global values, and even clearer about their radical character: "People have to see with new eyes and understand with new minds before they can truly turn to new ways of living. That is why global values must be the cornerstone of global governance."[51] As with WOMP, the Commission appears to derive its values from a blend of widely endorsed ethical sentiments and from ideas about how best to respond to a series of generally agreed-upon world order deficiencies. It also endorses, without even Küng's qualifications, the immediate agenda of the West: the spread of democracy and the virtues of market-driven globalization.[52] No attention is paid to justifying the metaphysical underpinnings of such values. There is a presumed secular rationalist consensus in support of such values, which are deemed as both sufficient and, in any event, the most that the postreligious mind is prepared to affirm.[53]

Küng indirectly challenges such secular complacency while welcoming a turn toward a global ethic that would reinforce his own advocacy. For Küng, the historical prospect of a global ethic is crucially dependent on enlisting the world religions directly in the mobilizing effort. Without such religiously oriented activism, Küng does not foresee a significant political impact deriving from either the positing of a global ethic or from the activism of transnational civil society. However, if churches, mosques, and temples around the world join in the effort, then the additional and complementary participation of various likeminded secular initiatives will hasten the process of implementation. The Commission's emphasis is almost the reverse. It seems to rely on the rationalist appeal of mutuality in a globalized world and on the democratizing activism of transnational social forces as embodied in a more globally structured United Nations and a more encompassing global rule of law, especially in relation to human rights. The Commission's essentially secular humanist vision never comes to terms with the tension between a "global neighborhood" and a world of increasingly unequal sovereign states, nor with the apparent contradiction inherent in its endorsement of economic globalization as currently practiced and its support for diminished economic disparities.[54]

Does Hans Küng Have a Vision for Our Era?
Prospects and Dilemmas

Given the complexity of the world and the elusiveness of change, it is difficult to evaluate the relevance of a given normative idea. Küng's general line of thinking seems to correspond with the ethical requirements of humane governance for the peoples of the world. At the very least, it provides a coherent framing of the issues relating to perspective and dialogue. As well, Küng's emphasis on cherishing traditional religious identities while discerning the core similarities with other religious traditions does provide a foundation for solidarity and stands against those in the West and the East that foresee the future as doomed to an era of intercivilizational conflict.

It is also helpful that Küng's outreach via the Parliament of the World's Religions, Global Ethic Foundation, and the InterAction Council is actively nurturing a climate of dialogue and issuing an urgent call to religious communities to participate in the lifeworld at this crucial historical time. Such a call, presupposing the relevance of normative and spiritual categories of meaning, challenges the economistic atmosphere produced by the ascendancy of neoliberal ideas about governance and the related social disempowerment of governmental institutions as a means to unburden the market by minimizing inefficiencies, thereby ensuring maximum economic efficiency. Küng's major effort is to reawaken a constructive religious activism while repudiating religious fundamentalism and exclusivist claims. This represents an important antidote to runaway secularism that is tied to the dynamic of uncontested capitalism as globally disseminated by a private sector media and Internet-dependent on consumerism for its own profitability.

Such a normative refocusing of energy is especially important in the wake of the collapse of socialism as a global political force and the overall weakening of organized labor. Capitalist circles were exhilarated by the outcome of the Cold War. Without the challenges of socialism and labor the capitalist ethos tends to adopt a cruel and socially complacent orientation. This orientation is not intrinsic to capitalism but is rather an opportunistic response to a perceived historical opportunity to maximize market autonomy. Such a tendency was reinforced by prevalent antiregulatory attitudes associated with a reaction against often heavy-handed bureaucratic control of business and by the pressures generated by acute competitiveness arising from the transnational intercorporate and banking struggles to gain global market share. These developments cumulatively have produced a process that might be described as the "social disempowerment of the state," which adds further to the problems of equity and empathy in a secular society organized along capitalist lines. In such a setting, only religious consciousness is widespread enough to offer a sense of an alternative perspective that seems capable of putting ideas of solidarity and compassion back on the political agenda. And only religion is universal enough to be resonant throughout the world.

At the same time, as Küng convincingly shows, that portion of the religious resurgence that centers upon a backlash to modernity mainly operates as a negative or regressive force. This type of resurgence tends to assume fanatical forms that intensify the destructive potentialities of nationalism, ethnic conflict, and oppressive state rule. Religious extremism is not a constructive antidote to the shortcomings of secularism, but just as cruelty is not intrinsic to capitalism, so extremism is certainly not intrinsic to religion. In this respect, Küng's idea is to reconcile robust religious engagement with the positive legacies of the Enlightenment, including its emphasis on reason and reasonableness, tolerance and moderation. Such features also resemble Küng's advocacy of the golden mean as the preferred way to address global issues.

Küng is equally clear about the irrelevance of a diluted religiosity comprised from a variety of pseudoreligions, based on the embrace of a syncretist amalgam of world religions and declared to be the new universal religion for an era of globalization. To be a vibrant historical force, religion needs to retain its rootedness in a series of particular traditions and beliefs that are delimited in distinctive rituals, parables, mythic tales, and prophetic messages. As with state structures, religious institutions often become ossified over time, their operatives being more concerned with bureaucratic stature and prerogative than with the spiritual and social wellbeing of their most disadvantaged members. Often the vitality of a religious outlook is better associated with subtraditions and countertraditions within each religion than it is with the mainstream orthodoxy. Küng's religiosity entails a high degree of responsiveness to implementing his vision of a global ethic as the North Star of the world, guiding and orienting those with responsibility for global governance.

Although Küng's assessment seems persuasive, it does contain some problematic aspects. For one thing, Küng purports to seek the minimum shared core values among the religions, associating this core with a thin morality that is devoid of the distinguishing beliefs and doctrines that are to be found in each particular religious outlook. As discussed, this leads to an operational emphasis on the golden rule and on treating each person humanely. The difficulty here is that if such widely shared ethical precepts are treated abstractly they seem irrelevant, while if regarded as the basis for judging action they appear to be too vague to have behavioral and policy implications. The global ethic in its generality is too easy an affirmation. If, however, such precepts were to be translated into action principles relating to behavior, then their implications seem too radical, given the distribution of power and privilege in the world as well as Küng's willingness to work with congenial representatives of the established secular and religious orders. It would appear intolerable to accept the extremes of wealth and poverty between regions, classes, races, and genders that currently exist and are being extended still further all the time.[55] It seems especially intolerable to neglect the needs of disadvantaged peoples who are living in destitution, without basic human needs such as food, water, health, education, and shelter. The existence of tens of millions of refugees and displaced persons, as well as political prisoners, would also not be acceptable.

In this respect, Küng's programmatic content for a global ethic seems flawed—it seems either an irrelevant piety or a utopian dream. As such, the question of agency is raised, of the social forces that might implement the global ethic in relation to the authority of the state and the market. In fairness, Küng addresses these concerns, mounting a strong attack on the prevailing realist orientation of the state, arguing the case for an enlightened rationalism that incorporates the global ethic. He makes a comparable argument against neoliberalism in the setting of globalization and in relation to the future of Europe. But the argument is essentially an appeal to the long-run self-interest of states and business elites. It does not encourage a collaboration among transnational social forces and more humanely oriented governments, a recent innovation that has had some notable successes, such as the widely ratified 1997 Ottawa treaty, prohibiting antipersonnel landmines; the Rome treaty of 1998, establishing an International Criminal Court; and the Kyoto Protocol on Climate Change.[56] This collaborative possibility, a so-called "new diplomacy," seems more promising than a mere appeal to governmental elites to abandon their realist world pictures.

Although impressively sensitive to the degree to which realism and neoliberalism challenge the prospects for realizing a global ethic, Küng does not succeed altogether in depicting the depths of the difficulty. It is not only a matter of questioning the realist premises of statecraft, it is also necessary to consider the consequences for the state of subordinating its policymaking functions to the discipline of global capital. When in early 1999 a clear social democratic mandate was given by the German electorate, it was expected and hoped that the new finance minister, Oskar Lafontaine, would be the person with the capacity to move German government fiscal and tax policy in a more socially oriented direction that was less subservient to business interests. In fact, this expectation generated intense postelectoral opposition to Lafontaine in business and financial circles, including threats of capital flight, that was so formidable that it led to his resignation in a matter of weeks after Germans had cast their vote, at once a slap in the face of democracy and a seemingly necessary step by the elected government to reassure the business world. Immediately, the stock markets signaled their approval by registering large gains, and the political waters calmed. The point here is that governments are not "free" to embody the global ethic, even in moderate forms by exhibiting a greater commitment to equity for their own territorial community, if they are perceived as interfering with market logic. It is not only that globalization has weakened the state, but, more decisively, that these economic forces and ideas have reoriented government, making it more accountable to the market and less to the citizenry.

There is also not enough discussion devoted by Küng to geopolitical factors that put the West in a hegemonic relation to the rest of the world or that make the United States a practitioner of hegemonic geopolitics despite its supposed identity as a state seeking to enhance the human condition. With a weak and weakened United Nations, it is almost inevitable that leading states will seek to provide for global security. With the collapse of bipolarity, the United States finds itself fulfilling such a role, but with extremely controversial results that cannot easily be seen as consistent with the implications of a global ethic. Also, the current American global leadership promotes the most unconditional forms of neoliberal capitalism, allowing market factors to take precedence over social factors, often leading to humanitarian catastrophe, as through the implementation of IMF structural adjustment programs. Since the late 1990s the Bretton Woods institutions have avowed a greater commitment to human wellbeing especially in the aftermath of the Asian financial crisis. It remains doubtful that these adjustments are of sufficient depth to challenge the neoliberal orientation of the leading international financial institutions. It is not to be expected that Küng would address these varied and technical matters in detail but that he would discuss them to the extent necessary to situate the project of achieving a global ethic within the matrix of contending political forces.

One final matter that bears on religious relevance: Küng is silent about religious activism, what I have called "engaged spirituality."[57]

This activism entails stepping forward in moments of crisis as a matter of religious conviction to oppose violence and injustice. Such exemplary action has certainly been taken in this historical period, becoming especially salient in the United States and Vietnam during the Vietnam War. The nonviolent resistance of two Catholic priests, Daniel and Philip Berrigan, was an important witness against their view of the radical evil of the American role in Vietnam. The self-immolation of Buddhist monks in Vietnam during the early 1960s was an even more powerful "cultural scream" in opposition to the war policies. It would seem important for religious institutions to view the forgiveness of debts to Third World countries, an initiative promoted in the Christian West by Jubilee 2000 as a major expression of religious concern for the wellbeing of those most disadvantaged. But there are other opportunities as well to awaken the conscience of secular society and to deliver the message that religion is committed to inclusive ideals of peace and justice: Religious leaders placing themselves on the frontlines between potential adversaries in warfare could be an immensely powerful impetus to celebrate and support the advent of a global ethic of the very kind that Küng is urging. It would also dramatize religion's tangible relevance to human wellbeing and humane governance and be of especial significance in relation to nonviolent security paradigms.

Küng, as much as any religious thinker of our time, has clarified the positive potentialities of inclusive religious engagement in addressing the shortcomings of the global lifeworld. This clarification, however, is not complemented by a credible politics of implementation. As a result, Küng's advocacy suffers from the humanist fallacy of believing that unjust structures can be transformed by appeals to conscience or by arguments directed at shifting the interests of elites. Such a pattern of reliance is naïve, as Küng himself demonstrates when he discusses aggressive threats directed as global security. In such circumstances, Küng accepts the necessity of reliance on countervailing power, up to and including war. Such an outlook is also needed to achieve an embodied global ethic, although the terms of struggle need not—and should not—be shaped by violence. The Seattle outbursts directed at the World Trade Organization in late 1999 are indicative of the kind of challenge that, if it expands and deepens, could prove to be the basis of a global political movement with a transforming potential.

7.
Gandhi's Legacy for World Order

What is the Gandhian Legacy?

Gandhi's successful challenge to British colonialism is viewed as a heroic anomaly in a world still generally interpreted through a "realist" prism that regards violence and hard power relations as the main causative agents of history while at the same time deliberately excluding moral and legal considerations as distractions from a rational decision process. Although the memory of Gandhi is revered everywhere, the life and ways of Gandhi have not often been treated as influential in relation to subsequent patterns of political practice, either within states or at a global level. Instead, there has been a widespread belief that what Gandhi achieved was unique to his time, place, and person. In this sense, what interest in Gandhi's ideas that persists has been limited to academic programs devoted to non-violence and peace studies, as well as the inspirational background of scattered activists and visionaries. There is some historical interest, as well, in the extraordinary role played by Gandhi in liberating India from the British Empire without reliance on guns and violence. Gandhi's method for dealing with a specific set of events in the past became almost a closed book as far as the political life of India and elsewhere are concerned as soon as Gandhi himself passed from the scene.

True, there were definite reverberations of the Gandhian heritage in the American civil rights movement a generation later under the leadership of Reverend Martin Luther King, Jr., but this struggle against racial discrimination was devoted to the implementation of the U. S. Constitution and a process of reform that never questioned the legitimacy of the established order. Besides, Gandhi seemed exotic, irrelevant, and too extreme for most of King's followers. Here and there political initiatives have been directly inspired and their tactics shaped by Gandhi's approach and life of dedication, especially those undertaken by individuals and groups with strong religious convictions. There was a kinship between Gandhi and King that arose from their intense commitment to a religiously oriented form of political practice.

In some cases, the struggles of many groups of religious activists against militarism and war, particularly in the United States, have been guided by a principled adherence to the unconditional nonviolence so vividly articulated by Gandhi's words and deeds. In this connection, I think of the writings and lifetime commitments of the Berrigan brothers (Daniel and Philip) and James Douglass. Douglass, together with his wife Shelley, founded Ground Zero (a community of religiously inclined activists determined to obstruct the deployment of Trident Submarines at a naval base near to Seattle, Washington during the 1970s and 1980s) and invoked the examples of Gandhi and Jesus to explain their course of militant action. Part of their seriousness came from meditating upon and studying the lives of these exceptional individuals. But unlike Gandhi's own experience, including that in South Africa, this more radical peace movement activity never managed to mobilize a mass challenge to war and militarism. However, Ground Zero's achievement should not be minimized. It indirectly influenced many in the mainstream, especially young people, during the long decade of the Vietnam War and during the nuclear arms race that was at the core of the Cold War. It was a largely symbolic witness. It was widely admired but never coalesced into a general challenge of the sort that Gandhi organized to overturn an entire structure of power.

I think that part of the distinctiveness of the Gandhian phenomenon lies in its embrace of an unconditional reliance on nonviolence to challenge, dismantle, and transform an entire structure of power and authority. It did so on an uncompromising basis of mass mobilization on the part of unarmed people, many of whom were trained to endure severe violence without striking back. Indeed, in this respect, Gandhi's core achievement in India has never been duplicated elsewhere. Even in India the sustainability of a nonviolent ethos was put in doubt while Gandhi was still alive by the outbreak of Muslim/Hindu violence, by the Hindu nationalism of Gandhi's assassin, and by Nehru's blatant and abrupt departure from the Gandhian path almost immediately after he became head of an independent India.

In effect, Nehru was willing to proceed down the nonviolent path that Gandhi cleared to confront entrenched and superior

British police and military power, but once he was on his own and India had achieved independence, he insisted upon and deployed the instruments of violence as practical necessities. By so proceeding, Nehru "normalized" the behavior of India as a state among states in light of the violent character of international political life. Gandhi's own views were that a commitment by India to a nonviolent statecraft would have a transformative impact upon the character of international relations generally.[1]

But recently the question of Gandhian relevance is being posed anew, yet not directly or explicitly, by a series of political movements that have emerged under quite diverse conditions and that suggest a major turn toward nonviolent forms of struggle by those advocating transformative change. This turn seems complex and contradictory, and it may not be sustained. Aside from its adherence to nonviolent practice, its general political line is essentially tactical, seeking to turn weakness into strength by engaging the enemy in a manner that minimizes the advantages of the militarily stronger side and maximizes its vulnerability to moral/spiritual challenges. Its relevance has been most evident in the struggles of civic movements of resistance against various forms of oppressive rule that rely on arbitrary and brutal violence and exercise control over the mechanisms of violence.

An important aspect of the current historical setting is the almost total abandonment of Marxism/Leninism/Maoism, which all posit as a tenet of belief the unavoidable necessity of armed struggle as active revolutionary ideology. This abandonment is the result of several connected developments, a process that has been especially accelerated by the Soviet collapse and the Chinese shift of attention to the dynamics of modernization in a highly marketized world economy. A further factor is the social learning experience of activists and radicals, who have understood both the potency of nonviolent struggle in an array of settings and the dismal disappointments of sustained armed struggle. Violent revolutions have led, in the end, to despair, or at least to compromises that might have been achieved far earlier in the course of a struggle if misguidedly romantic views about the prospects of revolutionary violence had not been accepted. Governments, too, have learned that their reliance on violence, even if they have a seeming overwhelming superiority in the use of forces, does not result in surrender or victory, but drives a weaker adversary to adopt more and more desperate forms of violence, a course of action that will not result in the restoration of stability. In the face of a determined political movement, one-sided peace imposed by the state is not likely to achieve its intended results of resolving the conflict and may well result in a renewal of anti-regime violence.

Another aspect of these circumstances that seems to be deideologizing revolutionary practice arises from the effects of economic globalization, especially its tendency to give priority to abstract targets of market shares and economic growth that can only rarely be directly achieved on a field of battle (arguably in the 1991 Gulf War).[2] This partial obsolescence of war is being reinforced by the astonishingly rapid growth of media and cyberworld influence coupled with the confidence that soft power modalities of struggle tend to be decisive under most contemporary world conditions, especially given the importance being attached to various symbolic battles over entitlements of opposed groups to political legitimacy. Such revolutionary challenges posed in the 1990s by the Zapatistas in Mexico and the Tupac Amaru in Peru have tellingly disclosed their preoccupation with the harmful impacts of globalization on the poor and vulnerable in their respective countries, and although not invoking nonviolence as an approach to their political struggle, these groups manifest a strong interest in finding new and less destructive ways to pursue their revolutionary goals and even rely on imaginative recourse to the global media and the Internet to tell their story. The main intention of such new revolutionaries is to gain sympathy in the world for the legitimacy of their demands and internationalize their grievances against the established order that exists within a particular country.

From these perspectives the last quarter of a century has exhibited an extraordinary range of militant political movements that have to varying degrees endorsed and practiced nonviolence. These movements have not been self-consciously Gandhian but have pursued a political course that appears guided by pragmatic assessment of relative strengths and weaknesses in particular contexts of struggle. The precariousness of their commitment to nonviolence is disclosed, to some extent, by the adoption of violent methods once the movement has succeeded in achieving control over the apparatus of state power and has shifted roles from that of being in a posture of resistance to that of being in charge.

Proceeding on the basis of a Gandhian ethos of nonviolence, how is the recent experience to be evaluated? There are two broad possibilities, with many variations in between. The first view would take an optimistic line, regarding these occasions of tactical reliance on nonviolent approaches to be exhibiting a trend away from the blind assumption disseminated by the realist mindset about the efficacy of violence. Gandhi was himself a kind of realist who viewed his own life as a series of explorations relating to truth-bearing (*ahimsa*) and courage and possessed an appreciation that some choices are so difficult that reliance on a degree of violence can be understood and even affirmed.[3] Gandhi's lifelong reflections on the teachings of the Bhagavadgita and its complex view of war and duty suggests the degree to which Gandhi understood the difficulty of repudiating violence unconditionally, despite his own deepening commitment to nonviolence. Gandhi's own approach stressed active engagement on behalf of justice, scorning passivity as being often a greater evil than violence as a response to acute injustice.

The second possibility is to view tactical nonviolence with skepticism, as a kind of impurity of means that is bound to taint the ends being pursued. In this regard the lack of an unconditional and principled commitment to nonviolence is likely to mean that violence will be relied upon as soon as the tactical realities are reversed, and to this extent the process that discredited Marxist/Leninist approaches to change will be reproduced with innovative rationalizations but no less bloody results. That is, if nonviolence is abandoned upon gaining control over a state, then a revolutionary politics is likely to become ruthlessly oppressive. Such conduct will no doubt be rationalized as a defense against counterrevolutionary forces.

With this background in mind, a few recent instances of tactical nonviolence will be set forth to provide some ground for making a choice between an optimistic and a skeptical interpretation of recent history from the perspective of a Gandhian ethos.

A Few Recent Instances of Tactical Nonviolence

There are a large number of examples that could be chosen as illustrative cases. Those presented here are selected because they appear to bear directly on the theme of inquiry relating to the Gandhi legacy.

The Iranian Revolution

In the mid-1970s a movement of opposition to the Shah's regime in Iran took shape, with its principal leadership being provided by an Islamic orientation articulated by Ayatollah Ruhollah Khomeini from his places of exile, especially Paris. This movement based its challenge upon a mass mobilization in the cities of Iran, especially Tehran, and was subject from its outset to brutal forms of oppression that included the repeated shooting of unarmed demonstrators and even attacks on hospitals and doctors who were trying to treat the wounds incurred by participants in these public events. Khomeini resisted calls in the streets for weapons ("Leaders, leaders, give us guns!") made by activists who were being subjected to an array of violent intimidations by the Shah's heavily armed forces. These state attacks culminated in a 1978 massacre in Jaleh Square, a public area surrounded by buildings in which demonstrators were trapped by soldiers firing machine guns from the available escape routes. Instead of firing back or changing the terms of struggle, the Islamic leadership, with impressive results, repeatedly urged demonstrators to put flowers in the barrels of guns and chant "[D]o not shoot, we are your brothers and sisters."

No theoretical grounding was offered in public, and after Khomeini returned to Iran in early 1979, the revolution that he led quickly moved in a violent direction, leading many prior supporters to allege that the scale and forms of its repressive violence soon exceeded that of the Shah so recently overthrown. Khomeini seems to have reined in the most vengeful tendencies of the new clerical elite in Iran, despite numerous executions and confirmed reports of torture as routine prison practice relating to enemies old and new, during his period of leadership. Nevertheless, without Khomeini's restraining influence the Baha'is might well have experienced a genocidal onslaught rather than enduring varying degrees of persecution and isolated atrocities. No longer was the political rhetoric couched in nonviolent language, but, on the contrary, the emphasis was on austerity and the punishment of evil deeds and disloyal acts. By the late 1990s the Islamic zeal had moderated, but there was no indication whatsoever that Iran intended to pursue its goals at home or abroad in a nonviolent manner. It has been reliably reported that Iran lent a large measure of support to an organization engaged in international terrorism and was itself seeking to acquire the capability to produce nuclear weapons. Arguably, from 1979 onwards the hostility of Iraq and the United States toward the Iranian Revolution created real and serious internal and external threats to Iran's political independence. But Iran's response led to a series of moves against imagined and real enemies that were based on extreme violence, ranging from the summary execution of critics to the deployment of young children on battlefields to detect minefields during the Iraq/Iran war. There was a total abandonment of the approach taken in the struggle against the Shah and no effort made to minimize violence, much less to avoid it.

In this context, then, the Iranian Revolution and its aftermath can be understood as having shown how effective nonviolent tactics can be in certain contexts of struggle, but also how fragile and reversible is the approach if it rests on exclusively tactical considerations.

People Power in the Philippines

A powerful movement took shape in the Philippines to drive the Marcos regime from power in 1986, a reaction in part to the assassination of a social democratic opponent, Benigno Aquino, and in part to the electoral fraud that seemed to epitomize the corruption of a brutal and venal leadership. There was great exhilaration in the Philippines, and important elements in the army backed the popular movement, with the United States standing aloof to avoid a repetition of its experience in Iran, where it found itself cast in the role of geopolitical villain and was accused of being both culturally decadent and politically exploitative. People Power eschewed all forms of violence, and its ascent to power was an exhilarating victory for democratic forces in a strongly authoritarian atmosphere.

But the victory was only partial. In Iran the old order was dismantled and its elite sent into hiding, put to death, or jailed; the governmental transformation occurred as the Islamic leadership promised, although it assumed a brutal form. In the Philippines, the energy of the victors was immediately devoted to reconciliation and reassurance, with the positive result that recriminatory violence was avoided. But neither was social justice achieved nor was the corruption of the old order seriously challenged. As with Iran, disillusionment followed, but the new path was relatively moderate, enticing many former armed revolutionaries to put down their weapons and play a peaceful role in Filipino society. The result has been a definite moderation of violence in the country but an acquiescence to the overall structures of inequity that has produced massive poverty and growing income disparities between rich and poor. Land reform has been stymied by traditional elites, and the military has remained a strong force in the internal politics of the country. Thus, the victories of People Power did not lead to an abandonment of nonviolence but rather to a co-option of the vision of a just society that motivated the movement. Nonviolence that is not directed toward social transformation forgets that the rationale for struggle and action is to overcome injustice; it cannot retain its true nonviolent identity if it reaches an accommodation with the sort of structural violence that involves economic misery for the many and glittering wealth for the few.

Eastern Europe, Especially Poland and Czechoslovakia

In Eastern Europe tactical nonviolence was an explicit response to the failures of violent resistance in the 1950s, particularly the experience of the Hungarian uprising of 1956 and the events in East Germany and Poland after 1958. New modes of nonviolent resistance were impressively theorized in the work of such intellectuals as George Konrad, Adam Michnik, and Vaclav Havel.[4] With the change in the Soviet Union brought about by the leadership of Mikhail Gorbachev and the vitality of mass movements of revolutionary opposition, the governing structures in East Europe crumbled from their own dead weight. When the puppeteer in Moscow no longer pulled the strings, the puppet slumped lifelessly; only in Rumania, ironically the country heralded in the West through much of the Cold War for its relatively great degree of independence from Kremlin guidance, was the entrenched elite willing to fight for its survival against its own citizenry.

What can be said is that movements such as Solidarity in Poland and Charter 77 in Czechoslovakia isolated and delegitimized governments that were long accustomed to ruling by force and intimidation and that were reinforced by Soviet influence and, as necessary, tanks within the Warsaw Pact area. Nonviolent opposition took many imaginative forms and was encouraged by external forces, especially by important links that were forged with peace and human rights movements in Western Europe during the 1980s. Such tactics definitely put the regimes in power on the defensive in a manner that earlier violent modes of opposition had been unable to do. The West could join in supporting claims advanced on behalf of human rights and democracy in a forthright way that was not possible when earlier movements of opposition relied on violence to achieve their goals of regime change. It was believed to be far too dangerous to intervene on behalf of movements seeking to wrest power forcibly from Warsaw Pact rulers and their Soviet handlers.

The fear of provoking World War III was a great inhibitor throughout most of the Cold War.

But again the victories of tactical nonviolence are partial at best. The rush of the new elites to establish free markets overnight has produced a wave of criminality, outrageous inequalities and corruption, and great suffering for large portions of the population. Ironically, in the face of these disappointments, citizens have been inclined in some instances to vote the hated Communists back into power, an astonishing reversal of the 1989 atmosphere. In other settings, the Catholic Church has substituted its authoritarianism for that of the former regimes, producing concrete setbacks for women and religious minorities. What can be said is that the tactical nonviolence as practiced in East Europe was too exclusively preoccupied with the transfer of power and was not able to reach a sustainable outcome with greater devotion to the attainment of a just society. It was not enough to be rid of communist rulers. A positive vision of a just society needed to be part of the struggle and was not.

The Intifada of the Occupied Territories

Here the movement by the Palestinians in the late 1980s arose out of a determined, yet spontaneous, attempt to find a way to oppose the violence of Israel, which was backed by overwhelming, often cruel force. The *intifada* was principled despite not adhering systematically and explicitly to a nonviolent approach. By unarmed Palestinians, including many who were young, taunting and throwing stones or even rocks at heavily armed Israeli occupiers, the brutality and illegality of the occupation was exposed as never before. TV footage revealed the one-sided character of the struggle as well as the Palestinian daily reality of impoverishment and isolation. The political impact of the uprising was to create and deepen cleavages within Israel itself, generating many debates as to the wisdom and acceptability of the occupation. The *intifada* also encouraged larger segments of world public opinion to comprehend, at long last, the Palestinian anguish and the justice of their call for self-determination.

A "peace process" of sorts ensued, with a Palestinian authority exercising control over limited portions of the Palestinian people in the West Bank and Gaza, providing education and social services in a system that was a counterpart to formal and official institutions. There was no Palestinian discourse that suggested overall dedication to a nonviolent orientation, even among dissident Palestinians engaged in peaceful activities. After the 1993 Oslo Framework of Principles began to be implemented, the glories of the *intifada* as a popular uprising were replaced by the bureaucratic corruptions and authoritarian character of the PLO leadership. In this instance, those who had been experimenting with and inventing new forms of oppositional politics were never allowed to exercise power. Their movement was reluctantly accepted by the official PLO opposition as "useful" in relation to the PLO's own quite conventional ambitions but discarded as soon as those ambitions were realized, even in fragmentary form, by the perks of partial control over portions of Gaza and the West Bank.

Pro-Democracy Movements in China and Burma

In these movements of the late 1980s, there seemed to be a definite principled commitment to nonviolent methods of political struggle and to the attainment of a democratic form of governance thereafter. Unfortunately, the failure of these movements to achieve their main goals has meant that the sincerity and capacity of these commitments has never been tested. Until power is held, adherence to nonviolence is not a good predictor of what will occur subsequently. Nevertheless, it seems clear that in Burma, at least, the convictions of the movement as articulated by Aung San Suu Kyi are indeed of a principled character and rest on philosophical grounds. They have also been maintained for over more than a decade.[5] It seems unlikely that such an outlook would be discarded if the movement found itself forming a new government. At the same time, whether a democratic orientation with support for human rights would lead to a pacifist approach to national and regional security is another matter. As the Indian case suggests and the Iran experience confirms, nonviolence in an internal struggle is no indication of a nonviolent posture toward external threats and challengers. Some small countries have adopted out of necessity or prudence a nonmilitary approach to their security as independent, territorial entities, but few have grounded such policy on a rejection of violence in their external relations. Costa Rica is a partial exception, explicitly embracing a nonmilitary approach to foreign policy and national security, as well as seeking to encourage such an orientation within the wider domain of Central America, which has been ravaged by armed conflict and intervention for decades. There is a rising trend of criminal violence within Costa Rica, and widespread reliance on heavily armed and private security guards does not convey a sense of a peaceful society.

Are We Approaching a Gandhian Stage of Human History?

At the very least, the ambiguous political instances just discussed, along with a large number of others, suggest that for the first time since Gandhi's death we can ask broader questions about whether or not an emergent Gandhiism is in the early stages of unfolding throughout the world. True, the concrete results are mixed, and overall not encouraging. There are numerous wars either underway or threatening in almost all parts of the world. Even Europe, which enjoyed its "long peace" throughout the Cold War, has had a series of wars in the 1990s arising out of the breakup of former Yugoslavia.

What is more, in Kosovo the effort to rely on nonviolent resistance under the leadership of Ibrahim Rugova gave way to the armed struggle mounted by the Kosovo Liberation Authority (KLA) in the late 1990s. The KLA did not attempt to take power directly, but did ensure that their violent action would provoke large-scale Serb retaliatory violence, which would arouse external public opinion. The main KLA tactic, which succeeded brilliantly, was to internationalize the conflict, inducing military intervention in 1999 by NATO forces. This violent intercession, justified as "humanitarian intervention," achieved de facto independence for Kosovo from Serbia, a result that could not have been gained by Rugova's nonviolent tactics. Part of the failure of nonviolence and the success of violence was a result of the external world being far more attentive to the latter than the former.

There are daily reports of brutality and recurrent eruptions of ethnic, state, and religious violence being perpetrated against women and children and against all that is innocent in many societies. The neoliberal ideology that accompanies economic globalization accepts no responsibility for the persistence of mass poverty and large-scale unemployment, while it regards incredible disparities in income as the acceptable byproduct of efficiency in the use of resources and as more than offset by economic growth over time. The end result of such priorities is that economic policy is capital-driven rather than people-driven, an economistic view of global policy.

And yet, the political trends observed contain seeds of hope that may yet produce a bright future for humanity. To begin with, there is the growing realization that war is generally useless or worse as an instrument of policy and, more broadly, that violence rarely succeeds either as a strategy for transformative change or as a means to sustain control. Of course, this realization is subject to some serious qualifications. On an international level, the Gulf War of 1991 and the Kosovo War of 1999 are widely interpreted as revindications of war as a policy instrument. At the same time, the deepening of the democratic spirit is leading courageous people throughout the world to experiment to different degrees with varying forms of nonviolence. This democratic spirit is broader than the embrace of constitutionalism in state/society relations. It encompasses grassroots initiatives by local and transnational action, as well as the overall emergence of global civil society as a political force.

There is also present a complex process of globalization from below in which transnational social forces are organizing in response to globalization from above under the aegis of global market forces.[6] These populist energies being unleashed are pushing hard in many different societal settings to support human rights, to help women in their quests for liberation, to bolster campaigns of environmental protection and debt relief, and to take on locally many other challenges that are being shaped globally. In particular, there exists for this evolving global civil society an ever-expanding and changing agenda of peace and development goals that include nuclear disarmament, reform of the World Bank and the IMF, and opposition to large dams and megadevelopment projects.

But should these various positive tendencies, which mostly remain at the margins of social and political reality, be associated with a kind of neo-Gandhian quest for peace and justice through the active commitment of women and men throughout the world? I think such an association, as one line of interpretation, is valid and suggestive of a potential future unity of direction for what otherwise might appear to be chaotic, futile, and random gestures of resistance against the overwhelming momentum being generated by globalization from above with its ideological coherence, its enthusiasm for consumerism, its indifference to suffering, and its reluctance to take steps to protect the global commons from destructive forms of overuse. The Gandhian heritage provides a coherent body of thought and practice that was evolved by Gandhi in the crucible of action and drawn from India's cultural and religious heritage and the sensitivities of their British colonial masters. It was powerful normatively and spiritually, and yet it encouraged creative responses to particular realities, always with an awareness that reliance on violence poisons means and ends and that its renunciation is quite consistent with maintaining and advancing concrete struggles for justice, however great the immediate cost.[7] For Gandhi himself that cost was the loss of his life through violence. It was a paradoxical slap in the face of nonviolent politics. Yet, it was also an expression of the religious depth of Gandhi's commitment, that is, unto death. Tragically, it also revealed the depth of secularists' contrary commitment to violent politics, and it is this commitment that has dominated India's regional role since independence. India's global role, arguably, retained some of the Gandhian ethos—the leadership of the nonaligned movement, which angered geopolitical managers in the West during the Cold War, and the consistent challenge to the premises and structures of great power nuclearism, which strongly criticized the self-serving nonproliferation emphasis championed by Washington. Any faint remnant of a Gandhian outlook for India was decisively put aside by the ascent to power of the Hindu nationalist BJP party. This new clarity contra Gandhi was underscored in the spring of 1998 by India's embrace of nuclear weaponry. Also notable was the enthusiasm in Indian civil society that greeted nuclear weapons tests, an expression of Indian nationalist pride but, more disturbingly, an association of this pride with a militarist initiative of great potential danger to the future of India and the region. Of course, the hypocritical censure of India (and later Pakistan) by the United States for daring to cross the nuclear threshold was an expression of global managerial concerns and not at all related to a belated appreciation of India's earlier antinuclear diplomacy.

Great changes in the pattern of human behavior normally occur when objective conditions, including prevailing ideas, change. War and violence, while remaining globally prevalent, are still gradually losing their charm as the dominant features of politics and history. Democratic initiatives premised on nonviolent militancy and an affirmation of human rights are helping to build global civil society on solid normative foundations. For these various reasons, then, it seems illuminating to connect this process with a Gandhian rebirth, although the historical results are so far quite ambiguous. In this respect, the Gandhian worldview essentially embodies a religiously grounded politics, informed by cultural tradition and sustained by meditation upon sacred texts. Gandhi's inclusive worldview, although drawing on Hinduism as an informing heritage, contrasts with the exclusivity of the BJP's reliance on an interpretation of Hinduism that is intolerant of other religious orientations. As discussed in the introduction and elsewhere this core distinction between inclusive and exclusive outlooks is embodied in the broad traditions of all the great world religions. Inclusive Hinduism reaches out to the world, whereas exclusive Hinduism banishes it.

8.

Our Millennial Challenge

The advent of a new millennium leads us, at the very least, to embolden the imagination. It is a marker thrown on the shore in the darkness of night while the river of history rushes by. We see no more and no less than what imagination allows, especially when it comes to our deepest hopes and most dreaded fears. This millennial passage encouraged extremes of expectation: the end of the world or the beginning of a new order. It is easier to indulge such speculations when the recent past is filled with either foreboding or a sense of great achievement.

The only prior millennial observance was essentially a European and Christian lamentation. Prevalence of disease invited religiously charged scenarios of the end of the world or of extraordinary divine intervention that would elevate humanity to new spiritual heights. Entering the twenty-first century, there is no assured or natural epicenter for millennial observation.

Early global village life confirms the existence of many voices clamoring to tell their version of the future. What we have gained by way of being universally wired, we may be losing by a stubborn sense of material conditions, cultural norms, historical isolation, and radical technological innovation. Thanks to the Cable News Network (CNN), people around the world have become more aware of the terrible ordeals of several black African countries; yet how distant most of us remain on the level of feeling or responsive action. And such awareness does not produce mitigating policies and responses unless prevailing ideas and practices point in an empathetic direction.

In an emergent empire of planetary scale, are we unknowingly and involuntarily becoming rootless subjects in a novel kingdom of consumerdom presided over by media lords, finance wizards, and dot-com billionaires? Or as individuals are we finally able to act as autonomous beneficiaries of electronic empowerment, enjoying the wonders of virtual reality that enable each of us to construct private utopias and convert fantasy to fact and fact to fantasy, without accountability to others? Or are we gradually becoming aware that this planet is too crowded and its resources stretched beyond carrying capacity, thereby reminding us of our ecodependence as a prelude to the most serious crisis of species survival in the history of humanity?

Indeed, are we preparing for such an urgent process of rediscovery of limits by loudly proclaiming the end of modernity and with it the end of the sovereign state and of our trust in science, technology, and reason as reliable guides for the human future? If so, what will come next: a glossy, glitzy postmodernism in which anything goes; a frantic revival of militant religion and many turns toward visionary cults that impose their will with relentless austerity and uniformity; a period of intercivilizational hostility, a new cold war that threatens us once again with scenarios of apocalypse; or, most likely, some ambiguous blending of these tendencies, allowing every fool and every demon to invoke the "voice of destiny" to claim an enthused following?

As Mark Twain so wryly advises, "It is best to read the weather forecast before we pray for rain." Yet, when it comes to geopolitics, the experts are not particularly to be trusted. They have turned out to be little more than "astrologers of power." Who among the trusted commentators in world affairs had the foresight to realize that by the mid-1980s the Cold War would come to an end? And who now can reliably foretell whether a nationalistic Russia will join an economically formidable China to threaten the West and whether Japan might shift sides in the future to tip the historic regional balance in Asia against the United States? Or who can tell whether by 2050 the danger of major warfare will recede from political consciousness or will be renewed in a regional format and conducted indirectly by battles between opposed robot, and even nanobot armies?

Does any given pattern of world order seem plausible at this point in time? It doesn't seem so; no particular image of the political, global future, including a persistence of present patterns, now attracts our attention. We do know the new millennium will bring drastic change, including dizzying technological innovations that will alter drastically what it means to be human. But we do not know what sort of response to anticipate: a rush to regulate and dominate or a currently unimaginable surge of humility and community arising from feelings of vulnerability and fragility. Our tools for understanding are too crude, while those of predicting are too weak to deal with the emergence of fundamental change. We need in the world historical situation the courage and dignity to acknowledge this ignorance and not be lured into a premature acceptance of a false certitude that presents itself as "truth."

But ignorance of the future does not relieve anyone from the responsibility of choosing a path of action or opening their eyes in the face of easily avoidable suffering. On the contrary, since little is precluded, much can be tried. We need to test many versions of the future for their viability and their ethical coherence. It misreads the present to be passive or discouraged. If our recent past bears witness to anything, it is that the "impossible" happens over and over again. Consider the ending of bipolarity, of the aggressive encounter of the nuclear superpowers; or the collapse of the Soviet Union into its constituent parts and the emancipation of eastern Europe; or the extraordinary transition in South Africa that brought Nelson Mandela, with the acquiescence of the main leaders of apartheid, from the prison on Robben Island to the pinnacle of government authority and international prestige. We are just beginning to understand why and how the impossible happens in the political sphere.

One source of insight is the study of complexity; another is chaos theory. In both, there is confirmation that dramatic outcomes can and do arise from trivial events. The flapping of a butterfly's wings in Chile induces a sequence of effects that results in a tornado in Oklahoma. Where were the butterflies that fashioned the end of apartheid? The explanation of these great surprises in history remain hidden from the view of our most accomplished specialists. What is accessible on the surface of events, the subject matter of analysis, almost always fails to disclose the future. Thus the impossible happens, for better or worse, and we go on, as before, pretending that rationality and our grasp of reality serve us well as guides to the future. Or, in the alternative, we follow blindly the lead of fools and charlatans that claim a prophetic insight into the future.

Yet the impossible does not happen accidentally. It reflects a play of forces that exerts pressures more profound than we realize, thus fashioning outcomes that are utterly unexpected. We should struggle to achieve the positive future we desire not because we have calculated that it can be achieved, but simply because others with well-defined projects are becoming organized and dedicated to the promotion of a destructive version of the future. Unless I act on behalf of my version, I make theirs that much more likely to happen. There is no reason to withdraw from the arenas of social and political struggle and ensure the triumph of adverse forces just because we can only accurately foresee the outcome after the fact.

I believe that the first calling of a citizen is engagement at points of interest and concern in improving the quality of life within the self, among family members, in the immediate community, in the wider social order, and in the global village. These concentric circles of allegiance, resembling the classic views of Aristotle and Rousseau about proximity and degrees of affection, are only a rough sketch, at most the beginning of a spiritual conversation. Such arenas of emotion, action, and exchange overlap and intersect within our experience and even more so in our imagination. They can be neatly separated into distinct categories only by the artifice of language. I have discovered that effectiveness as a citizen is rarely beneficial if conceived to be a solemn duty, but that the positive effects are far more likely to be greater if action is shaped by a sense of joy, satisfaction, and self-irony, as well as motivated by compassion and conviction. Such an assessment undoubtedly reflects the American scene, with its decades of stability, affluence, and ascendancy. It could not speak to a sub-Saharan African or a person of color in the Caribbean who has endured the immediacy of turmoil, acute poverty, neglect and despair.

Much harm has been done in the previous century by all-too-serious reform-minded, humorless individuals who thought they had all the answers and who tried, violently if necessary, to remove those who blocked their path. Much harm has also been done by those mired in passivity and a sense of fatalism in relation to the future. We should neither believe too little in our version of the future, nor too much!

Against such a background, we need energizing visions and dedicated leaders, but we must be exceedingly wary of truth claims, of violent means, and of intolerance toward others. There are certain aspects of this struggle for a better future that can be generalized in the form of norms or caveats. Reliance on violence to achieve political ends, for example, is rarely a means to improve things and has generally had a dampening impact on the prospects on managing change and historical breakthroughs. If this dawning millennium can foster a wider and deeper appreciation of the revolutionary potential of nonviolence, then the prospects for the global future immediately improve. This is especially true if we understand that the domain of politics operates at all levels of the social order, from the intimacy of the family to relations with distant, exotic peoples; from overcoming social injustice to deference toward our natural and cosmic surroundings. We need both a realization of the extraordinary opportunities that make desired transformations possible and a lively awareness of limits that avoids making excessive claims of control or indulgence.

Nonviolence, of course, includes the quest for dignity, not abstractly prescribed but embodied in the religious and cultural traditions of the world as well as tested by reference to agreed transcivilizational norms included within international covenants that set forth human rights as obligatory international standards. Nonviolence in political relations also implies accepting the rule of law as the framework for foreign and global policy, as part of what constitutionalism and cosmopolitan democracy may come to mean in the new millennium. This could lead to a renewed commitment by governments and other political actors to renounce the use of force in world politics unless it is legally permissible as a valid claim of self-defense and, in the process, transfer responsibilities and capabilities to regional institutions and the United Nations system.

To be politically sustainable, such a move needs the reinforcement of a new, nonviolent approach to international security, a United Nations that is itself purged of the war system and relatively free from geopolitical manipulation, expressive of a disarming world that renounces and eliminates weapons of mass destruction. The menace of nuclear war, and more recently biowar, are both means of frightening leading societies into supporting huge military establishments and culturally embracing omnicidal security options in the name of national defense. The willingness to exterminate an adversary by using such weaponry is a continuous comment on the lack of an ethical foundation for the formation of national and global security policy. When this absence is accentuated by the rise of market forces and an accompanying economistic approach to public policy, there is a further thinning of the legitimacy of a wider governing process that is taking shape as a byproduct of neoliberal globalization. These developments have ensued despite the spread of political democracy in the sphere of state/society relations, suggesting both the need to reinvent and globalize democracy to respond to the rapidly changing historical setting and the realization that the quality of democracy depends on orientations of political culture as much as on constitutional forms and practices. For instance, if the political culture is warlike and imperialistic, then its exertion of democratic pressures will generate belligerent and exploitative leaders and policies. Under such circumstances the restraint of democracy, conceived as the popular will, would be beneficial from the perspective of global ethics and responsibility.

Clearly, the reinvention of democracy is a growing challenge without historical precedent. States are losing their role as independent and creative actors on the world stage, and the instruments of elections and political parties seem less and less effective and meaningful as ways for citizens to participate in setting a national agenda. (Of course, a people finally emancipated from a long thralldom of authoritarian and oppressive rule finds excitement in the symbols and rituals of participation, at least for a while, as seems the case recently in South Africa and several Latin American countries.)

There are new actors associated with global market forces and informatics that are in free fall, operating subject to almost no authority and acting without accountability for wrongs done and the harm that results. The discovery of ways to participate and to hold business leaders accountable will determine whether or not the effort to reconstruct democracy on a transnational basis will succeed. The initiatives of women, indigenous peoples, human rights activists, environmentalists, antinuclearists, and others to build regional and global networks contain possibilities for the strengthening of global civil society and with it an effort to fashion new political forms that could, if successful, bring some type of cosmopolitan democracy into being by the middle of the twenty-first century.

Such a globalization from below offers a prospect of exerting countervailing pressures to offset the formidable institutional reality of globalization from above, which operates by way of the Bretton Woods institutions and the summit meetings of the industrialized states, as well as through an array of regional and private transnational economic associations.

My affinity with globalization from below is both partial and personal. It is partial because market forces, if framed by a regulatory ethos based on human solidarity and environmental protection, can provide the peoples of the world with choice, quality, the benefits of remarkable technological innovations, a rising living standard, and an elimination of economic misery. It is also partial because states and political leaders can exert their influence to rein in the destructive aspects of globalization from above, either by leading peoples away from pure secularism and materialism or by making sure that the disciplines of global capital are balanced by effective principles of human accountability that produce a sound equilibrium of regional and global scope.

It is personal because from the time I was a kid growing up in Manhattan I have sided with the underdog. In those days it was a matter of celebrating the generally lowly, yet colorful and feisty Brooklyn Dodgers, rather than following the perennial baseball winners, the pin-striped New York Yankees.[1] As an adult it has been a matter of identifying with the weak rather than the strong in the world and working on behalf of indigenous peoples and other peoples denied that most fundamental of all human rights, the right to life, which can be safeguarded only by the collective right of self-determination. Self-determination for a people is so fundamental because it provides the necessary social, political, economic, and cultural ground upon which individual human rights can stand firm.

In the United States for me and many others of my generation and those younger, the Vietnam War was as much a test of character as a time of turmoil and political challenge. It allowed me to understand myself in the mirror of the controversy that so deeply divided American society for more than a decade (while devastating the countries of Indochina!). It was a confirmation of my childhood truth that I belonged with the dissenters, the weak, and those being victimized and not with the rich and powerful, the policy makers and established order. But it also confirmed the borderless reality of empathy and human solidarity. And it confirmed my understanding of patriotism as demanding the citizen to act on the basis of conscience, and not to treat obedience and deference to the state as political virtues.

Of course, as a professor at Princeton over many years, my position and sentiments are inherently ambiguous. I am a privileged beneficiary of the established order with the security to indulge the impulses of my moral and political imagination. I realize this is a luxury for me as a person, but in my view it also allows me to play a more socially valuable role. A country as rich and powerful as the United States in particular needs independent critics at all levels of society. I am surprised that there are so few genuinely critical voices in the privileged sanctuaries of academe. It seems that most of those with the vantagepoint and knowledge to offer a range of independent voices either harbor ambitions to be called to the heights themselves or, deep within, are fearful that if they speak out they will be thrown out of the club, or at least be less welcome. And it is true that taking controversial views made me less welcome in the corridors of power and their social extensions, as well as within the confines of ivy walls.

My own position is also shaped by an interpretation of the historical setting. If writing in the late 1930s, for example, I suspect that I would have been preoccupied with the rising menace of militant fascism and the long shadows of the Great Depression. I feel the main threat today comes from global market forces that are eroding the independence of sovereign states and are operating without community ties or accountability, thereby endangering the wellbeing of many vulnerable sectors of humanity as well as subjecting the planet's life support systems to undue pressures. Related to the perils of economic globalization are a series of radical technologies that seem destined to undermine our sense of what it means to be human.

In opposition to these current developments are those who are victimized and those who work in various transnational gropings towards the construction of a global civil society, seeking to sustain life prospects for future generations. These underdogs eventually may succeed. In the meantime, they provide crucial resistance to the most malicious effects of globalization from above, whether they be setting the fuse of the population time bomb, turning away from the torments of sub-Saharan Africa, ignoring the homeless wandering through American city streets, or mindlessly assuming that technological capacities should remain autonomous creatures of private sector assessments. Our most important millennial challenge is to bring into being a balance of equity, prudence, creativity, and humility that would engender an era of what might be called "humane globalization."

For such an outcome to be realized, the apparent randomness and disconnectedness of the religious resurgence would have to achieve some kind of planetary convergence. The nature of this convergence cannot yet be prefigured, but it would involve a widely shared realization that the problems being generated by the current laissez-fare form of globalization is fraught with danger from the perspective of the sacred and spiritual character of human life. Only with such a rediscovered religious consciousness can a series of responsive political initiatives unfold. Such a future for humanity would be postsecular without being antisecular, postnationalist without being antinationalist. In such a climate, the state as the guiding mechanism for most lives would refashion itself to serve the cause of humane globalization. Although this visionary future has a dream quality at present, the alternative acceptance of current dominant trends virtually ensures a nightmare future. At such a crossroads I will follow the sign pointing to humane globalization, despite an awareness that the roadway is largely unbuilt and the plans to do so are not agreed upon.

Notes

Introduction

1. Quoted in Alessandra Stanley, "Greek Church Waves the Flag in Nation's Identity Crisis," *International Herald Tribune,* 26 June 2000, p. 5.
2. Orhan Pamuk, *The Black Book* trans. Güneli Gün (New York: Harper Collins, 1994), p. 183.
3. Perhaps the most prominent of such proposals is that of the Commission on Global Governance, contained in its report *Our Global Neighborhood* (New York: Oxford, 1995).
4. Hans Küng has been playing an active role for many years in promoting such goals. See chapter 6 for fuller discussion.
5. For a range of views on the breadth of the right of self-determination, see Wolfgang Danspeckgruber, with Arthur Watts, ed., *Self Determination and Self-Administration: A Sourcebook* (Boulder, CO: Lynne Rienner, 1997).
6. For an excellent assessment of the civilizational perspective as approached from the West, see Jacinta O'Hagan, "Conflict, Convergence or Co-existence? The Relevance of Culture in Reframing World Order," *Transnational Law & Contemporary Problems* 9, no. 2 (2000): 537–567; also Edward W. Said, *Culture and Imperialism* (New York: Knopf, 1993), especially the latter chapters.
7. I have been particularly inspired by the work of Ahmet Davutoglu and Chandra Muzaffar in moving toward this understanding. See such representative writings as Davutoglu, "Globalization and the Crisis of Individual and Civilizational Crisis," in *Globality versus Democracy? The Changing Nature of International Relations in the Era of Globalization,* edited by Hans Köchler (Vienna, Austria: International Progress Organization, 2000), pp. 185-2020; and Muzaffar, "Globalization and Religion: Some Reflections," in *Globalization: The Perspectives and Experiences of the Religious Traditions of Asia Pacific,* edited by Joseph A. Camilleri and Chandra Muzaffar (Selangor, Malaysia: International Movement for a Just World, 1998), pp. 179–90; also Sulak Sivaraksa and Chandra Muzaffar, *Alternative*

Politics for Asia: A Buddhist-Muslim Dialogue (Kuala Lumpur, Malaysia: International Movement for a Just World, 1999).
8. See chapters 1 and 4 for elaboration; the legal aspect of the post-Westphalian orientation is the subject of an earlier book, Richard Falk, *Law in an Emerging Global Village: A Post-Westphalian Perspective* (Ardsley, NY: Transnational Publishers, 1998).

Chapter 1

1. Hugo Grotius, "Prolegomena," in *On the Law of War and Peace* (New York: Bobbs Merrill, 1925), p. 20.
2. Hedley Bull, *The Anarchic Society: A Study of Order in World Politics* (New York: Columbia University Press, 1977).
3. See Myres McDougal and associates, *Studies in World Public Order* (New Haven, CT: Yale University Press, 1960); McDougal and Harold D. Lasswell, *Jurisprudence for a Free Society*, 2 vols. (New Haven, CT: New Haven Publishers, 1992); see esp. vol. 2.
4. Grenville Clark and Louis B. Sohn, *World Peace through World Law*, 3rd ed. (Cambridge, MA: Harvard University Press, 1966).
5. For representative works from WOMP over the period of its existence see Saul H. Mendlovitz, ed., *On the Creation of a Just World Order* (New York: Free Press, 1975); R. B. J. Walker, *One World/Many Worlds: Struggles for a Just World Peace* (Boulder, CO: Lynne Rienner, 1988); Richard Falk, *On Humane Governance: Toward a New Global Politics* (University Park, PA: Penn State University Press, 1995); and Ali Mazrui, *A World Federation of Cultures* (New York: Free Press, 1976).
6. But see articulate argument in favor of world government in David Ray Griffin, "Global Government: Objections Considered," in *Toward Genuine Global Governance: Critical Reactions to Our Global Neighborhood,* edited by Errol E. Harris and James A. Yunker (Westport, CT: Praeger, 1999), pp. 57–68.
7. A more obscure secular theme focuses on the European regional experience as a prelude to a "world of regions." Such an image, while more promising than world government, remains a dim and remote prospect at present.
8. The emphasis on "emancipatory religious and spiritual perspectives" is premised on a distinction between "inclusive" and "exclusive" interpretations of the meaning of human existence. Inclusive interpretations are nondogmatic, allowing moral and political space for alternative interpretations and worldviews. Exclusive interpretations are insistent that there is only one true path and that the embrace of alternatives is inherently false, immoral, and worthy of destruction.

9. For negative assessments of globalization see John Gray, *False Dawn: The Delusions of Global Capitalism* (New York: New Press, 1998); and Richard Falk, *Predatory Globalization: A Critique* (University Park, PA: Penn State University Press, 1999).
10. Whether this constraint is objective or "constructed" is beside the point. For helpful discussion see Grahame Thompson and Paul Hirst, *The Myth of Globalization* (Cambridge, UK: Polity, 1996). Also George de Martino, *Global Economy, Global Justice: Theoretical Objections and Polity Alternatives to Neoliberalism* (New York: Routledge, 2000).
11. The regulative mechanisms are subtle and elusive: the logic of competitiveness that exerts pressure on production costs, especially labor; the neoliberal orientation of elites; and the veto power exercised by financial and business sectors due to the mobility of capital. For further discussion see Paul Krugman, *Peddling Prosperity: Economic Sense and Nonsense in the Age of Diminished Expectations* (New York: Norton, 1994). For helpful study of variable state adaptations to the challenges of globalization, see David Held, Anthony McGrew, David Goldblatt, and Jonathan Perraton, *Global Transformation: Politics, Economics and Culture* (Cambridge, UK: Polity, 1999).
12. By "geopolitically managed logic" is meant the impact of political and economic power on terms of trade. Thus agriculture is protected in many developed, rich countries that preserve their cultural identity and political balance, but in a manner that distorts trade flows and hurts the agricultural exports of economically disadvantaged countries.
13. For helpful discussions, see contributions to "The Globalization of Liberalism?", a special issue of *Millennium* 24 (1995): 377–576. Also Yoshikazu Sakamoto, ed., *Global Transformation: Challenges to the State System* (Tokyo: UNU Press, 1994).
14. See Barry R. Posen and Andrew L. Ross, "Competing Visions for U.S. Grand Strategy," *International Security* 21 (1996/1997): 5–53.
15. The ebb and flow of U.S./China relations is partly expressive of a tug-of-war between the economistic worldview (the "new geopolitics") of the treasury department and the balance-of-power, statist worldview of the Pentagon. Of course, this is an over simplification of perspectives, a stereotyping of bureaucratic outlooks that neglects intrabureaucratic nuances and tensions. It also overlooks the Chinese role in shaping U.S. perceptions of threat and opportunity.
16. See Immanuel Wallerstein, *After Liberalism* (New York: New Press, 1995).
17. For documentation see United Nations Development Program, *Human Development Reports* (New York: Oxford University Press, 1990–1999).
18. See John Williams, "Look, Child Poverty in the Wealthy Countries Isn't Necessary," *International Herald Tribune*, 12 July 2000, p. 8.

19. See Vito Tanzi and Ludger Schuknecht, *Public Spending in the 20th Century* (Cambridge, UK: Cambridge University Press, 2000); see also interpretation of findings in Martin Wolfe, "The Golden Age of Government," *Financial Times*, 12 July 2000, p. 17.
20. For a valuable review of the ideals and undertakings of the Copenhagen Social Summit, see the volume reporting on the "Copenhagen Seminars for Social Progress." *Building a World Community: Globalisation and the Common Good* (Copenhagen, Denmark: Royal Danish Ministry of Foreign Affairs, 2000).
21. Stephan Schmidheiny and the Business Council for Sustainable Development, *Changing Course: A Global Business Perspective on Development and the Environment* (Cambridge, MA: MIT Press, 1992); also Richard Falk, "Environmental Protection in an Era of Globalization," *Yearbook of International Environmental Law* (Oxford: Oxford University Press, 1996), pp. 3–25.
22. See Daniel Archibugi and David Held, eds., *Cosmopolitan Democracy* (Cambridge, UK: Polity, 1995); David Held, *Democracy and Global Governance* (Stanford, CA: Stanford University Press, 1995).
23. This encounter is a major theme of Falk, *Predatory Globalization*, n. 9, pp. 127–36.
24. For eye-opening discussions see P. Kurzweil, The *Age of Spiritual Machines* (New York: Viking, 1999); see an essay by a founder of Sun Microsystems, Bill Joy, "Why the Future Doesn't Need Us," *WIRED* 8, no. 4 (April 2000): pp. 238–47.
25. Robert Jay Lifton, *Destroying the World to Save It: Aum Shinrikyō, Apocalyptic Violence, and the New Global Terrorism* (New York: Metropolitan Books, 1999); Mark Juergensmeyer, *Terror in the Mind of God: The Global Rise of Religious Violence* (Berkeley, CA: University of California Press, 2000).
26. See Stephen Toulmin, *Cosmopolis: The Hidden Agenda of Modernity* (New York: Free Press, 1990); R. B. J. Walker, *Inside/Outside: International Relations as Political Theory* (Cambridge, UK: Cambridge University Press, 1993); Hendrick Spruyt, *The Sovereign State and Its Competitors* (Princeton, NJ: Princeton University Press, 1994).
27. "Imperfectly" to the extent that national identities do not necessarily correspond with state boundaries.
28. See Immanuel Wallerstein, *The Modern World-System*, 3 vols. (New York: Academic Press, 1974–1989); Samir Amin, *Eurocentrism* (New York: Monthly Review, 1989); Samir Amin, *Rereading the Postwar Period: An Intellectual Itinerary* (New York: Monthly Review, 1994).
29. For example, see Bruce Russett, *Controlling the Sword: the Democratic Governance of National Security* (Cambridge, MA: Harvard University Press, 1990), esp. pp. 119–145; Bruce Russett, *Grasping the Democratic Peace for a Post–Cold War World* (Princeton, NJ: Princeton University Press, 1993); for critical view see Joanne S. Gowa,

Ballots and Bullets: The Elusive Democratic Peace (Princeton, NJ: Princeton University Press, 1999).

30. This argument is developed in Richard Falk, "Siege of State: Will Globalization Win Out?" *International Affairs* 73, no. 1 (January 1997): 123–136.
31. For further clarification see Paul Wapner, *Environmental Activism and World Civic Politics* (Albany, NY: SUNY Press, 1996); Ronnie D. Lipschutz, *Global Civil Society and Global Environmental Governance* (Albany, NY: SUNY Press, 1996); Richard Falk, *Explorations at the Edge of Time: The Prospects for World Order* (Philadelphia, PA: Temple University Press, 1992).
32. The work of Hans Küng has moved in this direction in recent years. See Hans Küng, *Global Responsibility: In Search of a New World Ethic* (New York: Crossroads, 1991), and chapter 6 of this book.
33. For a closely comparable revisioning of religious consciousness, see the important book by Charlene Spretnak, *The Resurgence of the Real: Body, Nature, and Place in a Hypermodern World* (Reading, PA: Addison-Wesley, 1997).

Chapter 2

1. Significantly, at this time there are various uses of the terminology of the "new medievalism" to describe world order, reflecting the rise of overlapping authority sources displacing the clarity of a "world of states." For an influential formulation see Hedley Bull, *The Anarchical Society: A Study of Order in World Politics* (New York: Columbia University Press, 1977); also, Andrew Linklater, *The Transformation of Political Community* (Columbia, SC: University of South Carolina Press, 1997). The use of "medievalism" as a metaphor for an emergent world order has not been extended to the revival of the religious state, but it could be, if qualified.
2. There are many postmodernisms, but in particular is the split between deconstructive postmodernism, which consists of radical criticism of modernist pretensions of knowledge and ethics, and reconstructive (or restructive) postmodernism, which seeks to nurture an emergent respiritualization of culture and society. For an excellent exploration along these latter lines see David Ray Griffin, ed., *Spirituality and Society: Postmodern Visions* (Albany, NY: State University of New York Press, 1988); Charlene Spretnak, *The Resurgence of the Real: Body, Nature, and Place in a Hypermodern World* (Reading, PA: Addison-Wesley, 1997); see also Chellis Glendinning, *My Name is Chellis and I'm in Recovery from Western Civilization* (Boston, MA: Shambhala, 1994); and David Ray Griffin and Richard Falk, eds.,

Postmodern Politics for a Planet in Crisis (Albany, NY: State University of New York Press, 1993).

3. For an account of this point stressing the influence of John Locke's *Letter Concerning Toleration* (first published in 1689; cited edition Buffalo, NY, 1990), see W. Cole Durham, Jr., "Perspectives on Religious Liberty: A Comparative Framework," in *Religious Human Rights in Global Perspective*, edited by Johan D. van der Vyver and John Witte, Jr. (The Hague: Klewer, 1996), pp. 1–44, esp. pp. 7–12.

4. See Natan Lerner, "Religious Human Rights Under the United Nations," in van der Vyver and Witte, Jr., *Religious Human Rights*, pp. 79–134; pp. 83–6; and p. 86, n. 3.

5. Arjun Appadurai, *Modernity at Large: Cultural Dimensions of Globalization* (Minneapolis, MN: University of Minnesota Press, 1996), pp. 27–47, pp. 178–99.

6. A wide-ranging commentary along these lines is to be found in the work of Hans Küng. See, especially, *A Global Ethic for Global Politics and Economics* (New York: Oxford University Press, 1998), esp. pp. 1–28. For assessment, see chapter 6 of this book.

7. See Samuel P. Huntington, *The Clash of Civilizations and the Remaking of the World Order* (New York: Simon & Schuster, 1996).

8. See Raymond Aron, *Peace and War: A Theory of International Relations* (Garden City, NY: Doubleday, 1966).

9. It was also a suspect move as the indictment was issued in the midst of the NATO air campaign against the Federal Republic of Yugoslavia.

10. For one account of globalization in relation to the state, see Richard Falk, *Predatory Globalization: A Critique* (Cambridge, UK: Polity, 1999).

11. Of course, this is a subset of a question about the future of the state itself. Related to such inquiries is a concern about the changing *role* of the state in response to globalization, and how this affects secular orientations. In this period, the legitimacy of the state is tied far more closely to its democratic public order than to whether it adheres to a secular tradition. Possibly, this stress on democracy reflects the rise of religiously oriented states and, more specifically, the rise of Islam, which rejects separations of church and state and of religion and matters of secular policy.

12. A. Soroush, untitled lectures delivered at Princeton University, 10–11 November 1998.

13. See Ernst Cassirer, *The Philosophy of the Enlightenment* (Princeton, NJ: Princeton University Press, 1951), esp. pp. 134–96, pp. 234–74.

14. Cassirer, *Philosophy*, p. 161.

15. Such is the essence of tragedy and struggle that has accompanied the breakup of former Yugoslavia during the 1990s. The future of Kosovo is illustrative of an unresolved dimension of this disintegrative process.

16. For illuminating discussion of the general problematique, with explicit reference to McNamara, see John Ralston Saul, *Voltaire's Bastards: The Dictatorship of Reason in the West* (New York: Free Press, 1992), pp. 23–5.
17. See Albert Speer, *Inside The Third Reich: Memoirs* (New York: Macmillan, 1970); Robert S. McNamara and Brian Van De Mark, *In Retrospect: The Tragedy and Lessons of Vietnam*, rev. ed. (New York: Vintage, 1996); see also Gitta Sereny, *Albert Speer: His Battle with Truth* (New York: Knopf, 1995); Robert S. McNamara, James C. Blight, and Robert K. Brigham, *Argument without End: In Search of Answers to the Vietnam Tragedy* (New York: Public Affairs, 1999).
18. See the important modification of Hobbesian realism in Hedley Bull, *The Anarchical Society: A Study of Order in World Politics* (New York: Columbia University Press, 1977), esp. pp. 23–52, n. 1.
19. For an expansion of this argument on behalf of a different possible modernism deriving from Montaigne, see Stephen Toulmin, *Cosmopolis: The Hidden Agenda of Modernity* (New York: Free Press, 1990).
20. Alexis de Tocqueville, *Democracy in America*, trans. H. Reeve (London: Oxford University Press, 1946), p. 235; see also pp. 238–9, p. 304.
21. See Huston Smith, *Beyond the Post-Modern Mind*, rev. ed. (Wheatley, IL: Quest Books, 1989), pp. 191–2.
22. Such a syndrome is brilliantly expressed by Orhan Pamuk in his novel *The Black Book* (New York: Farrar Straus Giroux, 1994), pp. 52–7, where he mentions the commercial disinterest in mannequins that had a Turkish look: "Turks nowadays didn't want to be 'Turks' anymore but something else" (p. 54); and goes on to write: "My father never lost hope that some day mankind would achieve the felicity of not having to imitate others." (p. 57)
23. For one line of interpretation that focuses on the changing role of the state see Richard Falk, *Predatory Globalization: A Critique* (University Park, PA: Penn State University Press, 1999), pp. 35–47.
24. As quoted in William Drozdiak, "Khatami Seeks More Than Words; Despite Warming Ties, Keys to Progress 'Solely in Hands of U.S.'," *International Herald Tribune*, 12 July 2000, p. 7.
25. See Appadurai, *Modernity*, pp. 6–9.
26. Ibid., p. 19.
27. See George Soros, *The Crisis of Global Capitalism* (New York: Public Affairs, 1998); and John Gray, *False Dawn: The Delusions of Global Capitalism* (New York: New Press, 1999).
28. See Richard Falk, *Law in an Emerging Village: A Post Westphalian Perspective* (Ardsley, NY: Transnational, 1998).
29. The papacy is often a troublesome issue for non-Catholics, as is TV and other forms of evangelism for a wide range of believing

Christians. The pro-choice/right to life debate also brings to the fore persisting tensions between exclusivist and inclusivist views of religious truth and social relevance.
30. See Richard Falk, *Human Rights Horizons* (New York: Routledge, 2000).
31. See William E. Connolly, *Why I Am Not a Secularist* (Minneapolis, MN: University of Minnesota Press, 1999).
32. Indeed, the advent of "smart" weapons has generated a new period of one-sided warfare. This reality was first evident in the Gulf War, where the casualty ratio was 1000:1 in favor of the U.S.-led coalition. It was even more pronounced in the 1999 Kosovo War, where NATO forces engaged in 78 days of heavy bombardment of Serbia and Kosovo without a single casualty. With long-range missiles, satellite guidance systems, weaponry of mass destruction, and submarines, the leading military powers can devastate any point on the planet with only a few minutes notice. Furthermore, there are no neutralizing or retaliatory technologies or tactics of resistance available to less sophisticated adversaries, except for recourse to random, isolated, and counterproductive acts of terrorism.
33. See Toulmin, *Cosmopolis*, pp. 45–87, n. 15.
34. This perspective is set forth in Richard Falk, *On Humane Governance: Toward a New Global Politics* (University Park, PA: Penn State University Press, 1995).
35. For a suggestive exploration of these emancipatory potentialities, see Joel Kovel, *History and Spirit: An Inquiry into the Philosophy of Liberation* (Boston, MA: Beacon Press, 1991), esp. pp. 197–237.

Chapter 3

1. For influential summaries from divergent perspectives, see Samuel P. Huntington, *The Clash of Civilization and the Remaking of World Order* (New York: Simon and Schuster, 1996); Robert D. Kaplan, *The Coming Anarchy: Shattering the Dreams of the Post – Cold War* (New York: Random House, 2000); *Our Global Neighborhood: Report of the Commission on Global Governance* (New York: Oxford University Press, 1995); and Björn Hettne, Andrås Inotai, and Osvaldo Sunkel, eds., *Globalism and the New Regionalism* (New York: St. Martin's Press, 1999).
2. For extended depiction along these lines see Richard Falk, *Predatory Globalization: A Critique* (Cambridge, UK: Polity, 1999).
3. See chapter 2 of this book.
4. See chapter 6 of this book for elaboration of Küng's approach.

5. This psychological and cultural challenge to the meaning of being human, and even to the primacy of the human species, derives from the prospect of technological capabilities superseding human capabilities via cloning, robotics, nanotechnology, and "spiritual machines." See Ray Kurzweil, *The Age of Spiritual Machines: When Computers Exceed Human Intelligence* (New York: Viking, 1999); Hans Moravec, *Robot: Mere Machine to Transcendent Mind* (New York: Oxford University Press, 1999); and especially Bill Joy, "Why The Future Doesn't Need Us," *WIRED* 8, no. 4 (April 2000): 238–47.
6. See Torbjørn Knutson, *The Rise and Fall of World Orders* (Manchester, UK: Manchester University Press, 1999).
7. See Yoshikazu Sakamoto, ed., *Global Transformation: Challenges to the State System* (Tokyo: United Nations University Press, 1994); also Joseph A. Camilleri and Jim Falk, *The End of Sovereignty? The Politics of a Shrinking and Fragmenting World* (Hants, UK: Edgar Elgar, 1992).
8. See Daniele Archibugi, David Held, and Martin Köhler, eds., *Reimagining Political Community: Studies in Cosmopolitan Democracy* (Cambridge, UK: Polity, 1998).
9. See George Soros, *The Crisis of World Capitalism* (New York: Public Affairs, 1998); also Robert Gilpin, *The Challenge of Global Capitalism: The World Economy in the 21st Century* (Princeton, NJ: Princeton University Press, 2000).

Chapter 4

1. This chapter is a drastic revision of a lecture (paper presented at the conference "Revolution, Religion, and World Politics" delivered at the College of St. Thomas, St. Paul, Minnesota, October 5, 1987).
2. For a profound probing of this theme, see Robert Jay Lifton, *Destroying the World to Save It: Aum Shinrikyō, Apocalyptic Violence, and the New Global Terrorism* (New York: Metropolitan Books, 1999); see also Mark Juergensmeyer, *Terror in the Mind of God: The Global Rise of Religious Violence* (Berkeley, CA: University of California Press, 2000). For a fictionalized and prophetic perspectives see Doris Lessing, *Briefing for a Descent into Hell* (New York: Viking, 1971); and Doris Lessing, *The Memoirs of a Survivor* (New York: Knopf, 1974).
3. For an excellent formulation of this turn from secularism and mainstream modernism, see William E. Connolly, *Why I Am Not a Secularist* (Minneapolis, MN: University of Minnesota Press, 1999); also helpful are Robert Coles, *The Secular Mind* (Princeton, NJ:

Princeton University Press, 1999) and Jean Bethke Elshtain, *Who Are We? Critical Reflections and Human Possibilities* (Grand Rapids, MI: William B. Erdmans, 2000). For a more drastic rendering of these themes, see William Irwin Thompson, *Coming into Being: Artifacts and Texts in the Evolution of Consciousness* (New York: St. Martin's Press, 1996).

4. For a general assessment, see Andrew Reding, "Seed of a New and Renewed Church: The 'Ecclesiastical Insurrection' in Nicaragua," *Monthly Review* (July/August 1987): 24–55; also Andrew Reding, ed., *Christianity and Revolution: Tomas Borge's Theology of Life* (Maryknoll, NY: Orbis Books, 1987). See also the statement by the National Directorate of the FSCN of October 7, 1980, "The Role of Religion in the New Nicaragua," in Tomas Borge et al., *Sandinistas Speak* (New York: Pathfinder Press, 1982). A useful firsthand account is Joll Millman, "Nicaragua's Social Revolution Rests Largely on Scripture and Christian Base Communities," *In These Times* (24 February–8 March 1988): 22, 112–13.

5. This focus is developed powerfully by Upendra Baxi in "Taking Suffering Seriously: Social Action Litigation Before the Supreme Court of India," *Delhi Law Review* 91 (1979–80): 8–9. See also Baxi's *Courage, Craft and Contention: The Indian Supreme Court in the Eighties* (Bombay, India: N. M. Tripath, 1985).

6. See Anthony Arnove, ed., *Iraq Under Siege: The Deadly Impact of Sanctions and War* (Cambridge, MA: South End, 2000); more generally see David Cartright and George A. Lopez, eds., *The Sanctions Decade: Assessing UN Strategies in the 1990s* (Boulder, CO: Lynne Rienner, 2000).

7. Cf. A.G. Mojtabai, *Blessed Assurance: At Home with the Bomb in Amarillo, Texas* (Boston: Houghton Mifflin, 1986).

8. Sharon D. Welch, *Communities of Resistance and Solidarity: A Feminist Theology of Liberation* (Maryknoll, NY: Orbis Books, 1985).

9. Gregory Bateson, *Mind and Nature: A Necessary Unity* (New York: Bantam, 1979), pp. 8–10.

10. Poem "Revolution in the Revolution in the Revolution" in Gary Snyder, *Regarding Wave* (New York: New Direction Books, 1970), p. 39.

11. For ethical and legal rationales, see Christopher Stone, *Earth and Other Ethics: The Case of Moral Pluralism* (New York: Harper and Row, 1987).

12. Philip Shabecoff, "France Must Pay Greenpeace $8 Million in Sinking of Ship," *New York Times*, 3 October 1987, sec. 1, A2.

13. See Petra Kelly, *Fighting for Hope* (Boston: South End Press, 1984); and Petra Kelly and Rudolf Bahro, *Building the Green Movement* (Philadelphia: New Society, 1986); see also the report of tension

among the German Greens in Serge Schmemann, "For Germany's Greens, Success Breeds a Schism," *New York Times*, 11 October 1987, p. 22.

14. For a convenient summary of the Green perspective, see Charlene Spretnak, *The Spiritual Dimension of Green Politics* (Santa Fe, N.M.: Bear and Co., 1986), pp. 78–82.
15. For excellent information on India, see the regularly published issues of the independent newsletter *Lokoyan Bulletin*, published in Delhi, India under the editorship of Smitu Kothari and Harsh Sethi.
16. See Richard Shaull, *Naming the Idols: Biblical Alternatives for U.S. Foreign Policy* (Oak Park, IL: Meyer-Stone Books, 1988).
17. See Zsuzsa Hegedus, "The Challenge of the Peace Movement: Civilian Security and Civilian Emancipation," in *Towards a Just World Order*, edited by Saul H. Mendlovitz and R. B. J. Walker (London: Butterworths, 1987), pp. 191–210.
18. For intriguing speculations along these lines with some scientific foundations, see J. E. Lovelock, *Gaia: A New Look at Life on Earth* (New York: Oxford University Press, 1979).
19. See my earlier essay, Richard Falk, "In Pursuit of the Postmodern," in *Spirituality and Society: Postmodern Visions*, edited by David Ray Griffin (Albany, NY: State University of New York Press, 1988), pp. 81–98; appearing in altered form in this volume as chapter 4.
20. The fundamentalist option can be considered an *inappropriate* religious awakening that is quite likely to present a major challenge in the years ahead, especially given the uncertainties associated with this multifaceted process of transition from modernism to postmodernism. For one line of creative response to this moment of unfolding possibilities, see William Irwin Thompson, *Darkness and Scattered Light: Four Talks on the Future* (New York: Doubleday, 1978).
21. The practical and theoretical implications of this conjoined vision are explored in R. B. J. Walker, *One World/Many Worlds* (Boulder, CO: Lynne Rienner, 1988).
22. One suggestive line of thinking is to be found in Ronnie D. Lipschutz, *After Authority: War, Peace, and Global Politics in the 21st Century* (Albany, NY: State University of New York Press, 2000); see also Richard Falk, *Explorations at the Edge of Time: The Prospects for World Order* (Philadelphia: Temple University Press, 1992); and Jeremy Brecher, Tim Costello, and Brendan Smith, *Globalization from Below: The Power of Human Solidarity* (Cambridge, MA: South End Press, 2000).
23. Among many accounts see Zygmunt Bauman, *Globalization: The Human Consequences* (Cambridge, UK: Polity Press, 1998). Also, Jan Nederveen Pieterse, ed., *Global Futures: Shaping Globalization* (London: Zed, 2000); David Held, Anthony McGrew, David Goldblatt and Jonathan Perraton, *Global Transformations: Politics,*

Economics and Culture (Cambridge, UK: Polity, 1999); and Hazel Henderson, *Beyond Globalization: Shaping a Sustainable Global Economy* (West Hartford, CT: Kumarian Press, 1999).

Chapter 5

1. Jean Baudrillard, *Revenge of the Crystal* (Concord, MA: Pluto Press, 1990), p. 34.
2. I owe this distinction and outlook on postmodernism to a series of "Portrack Seminars," annual discussions in the early 1990s on postmodern themes, and especially to the core participants who were David Ray Griffin, Charles Jencks, and Charlene Spretnak.
3. On the character of global civil society see Richard Falk, "Global Civil Society: Perspectives, Initiatives, Movements," *Oxford Development Studies* 26, no. 1 (1998): 99–110.
4. For a trenchant critique along these lines see Noam Chomsky, *The New Military Humanism: Lessons from Kosovo* (Monroe, ME: Common Courage Press, 1999).
5. See also chapter 7 of this book.
6. For background, see Mahatma Gandhi, *An Autobiography: The Story of My Experiments with Truth* (Boston, MA: Beacon Press, 1957); and Richard G. Fox, *Gandhian Utopia: Experiments with Culture* (Boston, MA: Beacon Press, 1989).
7. For the most authoritative account of the Nuremberg Principles see Telford Taylor, *The Anatomy of the Nuremberg Trials* (New York: Knopf, 1992). For an innovative discussion of the Nuremberg conception in post-Nuremberg settings of liberal America, see Francis Anthony Boyle, *Defending Civil Resistance Under International Law* (Dobbs Ferry, NY: Transnational Publishers, 1987). General background materials can be found in Richard Falk, Gabriel Kolko, and Robert Jay Lifton, eds., *Crimes of War* (New York: Random House, 1971), esp. pp. 73–176.
8. Note that this shifts the relations of law and politics from a posture of justified disobedience to one of lawful obedience enforced by agents of civil society.
9. India and Pakistan are also de facto members of the nuclear weapons club, as is Israel, although it remains unwilling to claim or affirm such a status.
10. The deadline was contained in the key U.N. document, Security Council Resolution 678, Nov. 29, 1990.
11. Autonomy suggests independence. It is not meant to endorse a religious veto over political policy, as is the case in a theocratic state

such as Iran's Islamic Republic. It is meant to bring spiritual consciousness to bear on matters that concern human destiny, especially collective choices with great consequences that entail reliance on violence. Of course, the outlook of spiritual leaders varies, and endorsing their role in encouraging nonviolence implies tolerating their role in supporting right to life, capital punishment, and the like. The position argued is that, on balance, we need to reconnect the political with the spiritual as part of the effort to blur boundaries and to overcome the destructive aspects of the Enlightenment heritage: its sharp polarities between public and private, church and state, reason and emotion, good and evil, and even man and woman. A more androgynous overall identity is to be preferred.

12. The signposts along the way to postmodernism are helpfully addressed in David Harvey, *The Condition of Postmodernity* (Oxford, UK: Basil Blackwell, 1989); Charles Jencks, *What is Post-Modernism?*, 3rd rev. ed. (New York: St. Martin's Press, 1989); and David Ray Griffin's series on constructive postmodern thought published in the years since 1990 by SUNY Press, especially Griffin, ed., *Spirituality and Society: Postmodern Visions* (Albany, NY: SUNY Press, 1988). It should be noted that this essay writes of "reconstructive" postmodernism whereas Griffin describes a comparable orientation as "constructive" postmodernism. I prefer reconstructive, partly because it is more opposite to deconstructive postmodernism and partly because it is a matter of reconstructing, given past constructions. By reference to content, there is a definite affinity between Griffin's conception and my own.

13. On contingency as at the core of language, thought, and argument, see Richard Rorty, *Contingency, Irony, and Solidarity* (Cambridge, UK: Cambridge University Press, 1989).

14. Of the great world religions, Hindu metaphysics is, perhaps, clearest in its capacity to depict polarities in a spirit of noncontradiction.

15. For wide-ranging inquiry into the nature and tendencies of political allegiance, see Peter A. Furia, "Patterns of Allegiance: An Empirical Analysis of Group Identity and International Relations" (Ph.D. diss., Princeton University, July 2000).

16. See generally Richard Falk, "The Right of Self-Determination Under International Law: The Coherence of Doctrine Versus the Incoherence of Experience," in *Self Determination and Self-Administration A Sourcebook*, edited by Wolfgang Danspeckgruber and Arthur Watts (Boulder, CO: Lynne Rienner, 1997), pp. 47–78.

17. For a useful critical assessment of the emergence of modernity, see Stephen Toulmin, *Cosmopolis: The Hidden Agenda of Modernity* (New York: Free Press, 1990); and Trinh T. Minh-ha, *Framer Framed* (New York: Routledge, 1992).

18. The 1999 NATO war over Kosovo carried this process further. Relying on high altitude bombing patterns, NATO managed an intensive 78-day campaign without a single casualty to its military forces.
19. For general assessment, see Mary Kaldor, *New and Old Wars* (Cambridge, UK: Polity, 1999).
20. For a seminal consideration of cosmopolitan democracy, see David Held, "Democracy: From City-States to a Cosmopolitan Order?" in *Prospects for Democracy* (Cambridge, UK: Polity Press, 1993), pp. 14–52. For foundational work on the values of human dignity, see Harold D. Lasswell and Myres S. McDougal, *A Jurisprudence for a Free Society*, 2 vols. (New Haven, CT: Yale University Press, 1992).
21. See Richard Falk, *Explorations at the Edge of Time* (Philadelphia, PA: Temple University Press, 1992).
22. Part IV of Adrienne Rich, "Through Corralitos Under Rolls of Cloud," in *An Atlas of the Difficult World: Poems 1988 – 1991* (New York: Norton, 1991), p. 47.

Chapter 6

1. On fragmentation/globalization see Ian Clark, *Globalization and Fragmentation: International Relations in the Twentieth Century* (New York: Oxford University Press, 1997). For a broader view of these contradictory pulls in the evolving global setting, see James N. Rosenau, *Turbulence in World Politics: A Theory of Change and Continuity* (Princeton, NJ: Princeton University Press, 1990); and Joseph A. Camilleri and Jim Falk, *The End of Sovereignty? The Politics of a Shrinking and Fragmenting World* (Hants, England: Edward Elgar, 1992). A recent assessment of these developments is found in a paper by Ronnie Lipschutz, "Regulation for the Rest of Us: Global Civil Society and the Democratization of Global Politics," (paper presented at Rutgers University Workshop of Center for Global Change and Governance and the World Order Models Project, Newark, N.J., June 4–5, 1999).
2. Hans Küng, *A Global Ethic for Global Politics and Economics* (New York: Oxford University Press, 1998). Italics are used in quotations only when they appear in Küng's book. For a recent formulation by Küng, see "Global Ethic in Foreign Politics: The Middle Way between Real Politics and Ideal Politics" (lecture at Fordham University, Bronx, N.Y., Feb. 18, 1999). Küng's earlier call for a global ethic is contained in *Global Responsibility: In Search of a New World Ethic* (New York: Crossroad, 1991). Finally, note should be taken of the existence in Tübingen of a Global Ethic Foundation for intercultural and interreligious research, education, and encounter,

founded in 1995 to implement an outlook that appears to be inspired by Hans Küng.
3. In a broader sense, although without any direct explication, the realization of a global ethic at the level of practice in international life would contribute significantly to the achievement of what I have called "humane governance." See Richard Falk, *On Humane Governance: Toward a New Global Politics* (University Park, PA: Penn State University Press, 1995).
4. Küng's outlook embodies the emergent reality of overlapping loyalties and multiple citizenship. In a prefatory note Küng reflects on the outlook of the book, suggesting that "its approach should be attributed less to my origin in the country of William Tell than to my advanced age." (*A Global Ethic*, p. xvi) For exploration of changing identity patterns and the idea of citizenship, see Richard Falk, "The Making of Global Citizenship" in *The Condition of Citizenship*, edited by Bart van Steenbergen (London, UK: SAGE Publications, 1994), pp. 127–40.
5. The conceptual background is closely linked to the idea of sovereignty as the basis of community, generating boundaries between "we" and "they" as well as between "inside" and "outside" that have been crucial in the development of international relations theory. This theme is best explored in R. B. J. Walker, *Inside/Outside: International Relations as Political Theory* (Cambridge, UK: Cambridge University Press, 1993). For a more cosmopolitan outlook that draws on Stoic philosophy, see Martha C. Nussbaum, *Cultivating Humanity: A Classical Defense of Reform in Liberal Education* (Cambridge, MA: Harvard University Press, 1997), esp. pp. 50–84. Also see Martha C. Nussbaum, "Patriotism and Cosmopolitanism" in *For Love of Country*, edited by Joshua Cohen (Boston: Beacon, 1996), pp. 2–17. The sense of the locus of loyalty and identity is highly contested. See other essays in the same book, by Kwame Anthony Appiah, "Cosmopolitan Patriots," pp. 21–29; Amy Gutman, "Democratic Citizenship," pp. 66–71; Michael Walzer, "Spheres of Affection," pp. 125–27; and Nussbaum's response, "Reply," pp. 131–44.
6. Küng, *A Global Ethic*, p. xiii. Italics in original.
7. Ibid., pp. xiii–xiv.
8. Ibid., p. xiv.
9. For an illuminating assessment of such a prospect, see Mary Kaldor, *New and Old Wars: Organized Violence in a Global Era* (Cambridge, UK: Polity, 1999); see also Beverly Crawford and Ronnie Lipschutz, eds., *The Myth of Ethnic Conflict: Politics, Economics, and "Cultural Violence"* (Berkeley, CA: University of California Press, 1998).
10. Küng, *A Global Ethic*, p. 17.

11. Henry Kissinger, *Diplomacy* (New York: Simon and Schuster, 1994).
12. Küng, *A Global Ethic*, p. 7.
13. Ibid., p. 7. Italics in original.
14. Ibid., p. 9.
15. Ibid., pp. 10–11.
16. Walter Isaacson, *Kissinger: A Biography* (New York: Simon and Schuster, 1992), p. 13. In my view both lines of thought (that power relations are the main determinant of historical change and that competing moral ideas provide the decisive agency for global change) overlook what seems to have been the proximate and principle cause of the Soviet collapse: a rigid internal bureaucratic structure that was unable to keep pace technologically with the West and could not participate successfully in the world economy. For interpretation along these lines, see Manuel Castels, *The Information Age—Economy Society and Culture—End of Millennium*, vol. 3 (Malden, MA: Blackwells, 1998), pp. 4–69.
17. Such a view is persuasively argued in Torbjørn L. Knutsen, *The Rise and Fall of World Orders* (Manchester, UK: Manchester University Press, 1998).
18. Küng, *A Global Ethic*, p. 19.
19. See also the somewhat parallel questioning by Stephen Toulmin, who sets up the modernist crossroads with Descartes representing the road taken and Montesquieu the road not taken and argues that the role of reason might have been much less dogmatic had Montesquieu prevailed. See Stephen Toulmin, *The Hidden Agenda of Modernity* (New York: Free Press, 1990).
20. Küng, *A Global Ethic*, p. 20.
21. On the importance of Grotius in relation to the normative (moral and legal) transition from medievalism to modernity, see Richard Falk, *Law in an Emerging Global Village: A Post–Westphalian Perspective* (Ardsley, NY: Transnational Publishers, 1998). See also Hedley Bull, Benedict Kingsbury and Adam Roberts, eds., *Hugo Grotius and International Relations* (Oxford, UK: Clarendon Press, 1990); Yasuaki Onuma, ed., *A Normative Approach to War: Peace, War, and Justice in Hugo Grotius* (Oxford, UK: Clarendon Press, 1993). Elsewhere, Küng credits Max Weber and Hans Jonas for identifying and advocating this middle path. (*A Global Ethic*, p. 65)
22. Kung's recent focus on the middle way emphasizes a policy domain between Machiavellian/Kissingerian realism and Wilsonian utopianism, what is often associated in American political thought with "liberal internationalism." (See Küng, "Global Ethic") For an influential formulation, see Stanley Hoffmann, *Duties Beyond Borders: On the Limits and Possibilities of Ethical International Politics* (Syracuse, NY: Syracuse University Press, 1981).
23. Küng, *A Global Ethic*, p. 29.

24. Ibid., p. 65.
25. Ibid., p. 29.
26. Ibid., p. 33.
27. By conferring a veto on the five permanent members of the Security Council, the charter acknowledges its inability to provide security in the event that one of these leading states opposes the proposed course of action. Also, the member states have never endowed the organization with peacekeeping forces, sufficient funding, and the sort of logistical capacity needed to offer effective protection to targets of aggression. The charter both reaffirms the sovereign equality of states and defers to the primacy of geopolitics in shaping world politics on matters of strategic concern.
28. Ibid., p. 36. In effect, Küng is himself a realist to the extent of resting global security on the reliable enforcement of norms and prohibiting recourse by states to aggressive uses of force.
29. Ibid., p. 66.
30. Ibid., p. 92.
31. Ibid., pp. 92–3.
32. Ibid., p. 95.
33. Ibid., p. 95. Küng also invokes Max Huber's ideas of a weltethos, "basic common factors," among religions. See Michael Walzer, *Thick and Thin: Moral Argument at Home and Abroad* (Notre Dame, IN: Notre Dame University Press, 1994).
34. Küng, *A Global Ethic*, p. 110.
35. Ibid., p. 111. Italics in original.
36. For representative perspectives that share a normative kinship with Küng's advocacy of a global ethic, the Commission on Global Governance, see *Our Global Neighborhood* (New York: Oxford University Press, 1995); Kennedy Graham, ed., *The Planetary Interest* (New Brunswick, NJ: Rutgers University Press, 1999); and Saul H. Mendlovitz, ed., *On the Creation of a Just World Order* (New York: Free Press, 1975).
37. Küng, *A Global Ethic*, p. 132. I use the word "alleged" because I disagree strongly with Küng's assessment here. Although the emergence of human rights in recent decades is an encouraging development, it has not in any serious sense displaced the primacy of geopolitical or economistic factors in the execution of foreign policy by major states. Such a displacement would be entirely at odds with the prevailing neoliberal and realist climate of ideas.
38. Ibid., p. 133.
39. Ibid., p. 133.
40. Ibid., p. 138.
41. Ibid., p. 140.
42. Ibid., p. 141.
43. Ibid., pp. 220–76.

44. Hans Jonas, *The Imperative of Responsibility: In Search of an Ethics for the Technological Age* (Chicago: University of Chicago Press, 1984), p. 6.
45. Ibid., p. x.
46. Ibid., p. x.
47. For various WOMP formulations, see Saul H. Mendlovitz, ed., *On the Creation of a Just World Order*, n. 36; for more recent efforts see R. B. J. Walker, *One World, Many Worlds: Struggles for a Just World Peace* (Boulder, CO: Lynne Rienner, 1988) and Richard Falk, *On Humane Governance: Toward a New Global Politics*, n. 3.
48. See Küng, *A Global Ethic*, n. 2, p. 48.
49. Ibid.
50. Ibid., pp. 48–9.
51. Ibid., p. 47.
52. For a more critical account of globalization that also emanates from ethical concerns about the future of global society, see Jacques Baudot, ed., *Building a World Community: Globalization and the Common Good* (Copenhagen: Royal Danish Ministry of Foreign Affairs, 2000).
53. For a more complex view of interacting conceptions of values, see Alasdair Macintyre, *Three Rival Visions of Moral Inquiry* (London, UK: Duckworth, 1990).
54. For an analysis along these lines, essentially criticizing the commissions's orientation as insufficiently radical to provide a political foundation for its reformist proposals, see Richard Falk, "Liberlism at the Global Level: The Last of the Independent Commissions?" *Millennium* 24, no. 3 (1995): 563–76.
55. For data and analysis relating to income and wealth gaps, see especially annual volumes under the auspices of the United Nations Development Program, *Human Development Report 1997* (New York: Oxford University Press, 1997).
56. For amplification, see Richard Falk and Andrew C. Strauss, "On the Creation of a Global Peoples Assembly: Legitimacy and the Power of Popular Sovereignty," *Stanford Journal of International Law* 36 (no. 2): 191–219 (2000).
57. See chapter 5 of this book.

Chapter 7

1. See helpful interpretation of Gandhi's views on these matters in Rashmi-Sudha Puri, *Gandhi on War and Peace* (New York: Praeger, 1987), esp. pp. 224–28.

2. See John Mueller's *Retreat from Doomsday: The Obsolescence of Major War* (New York: Basic Books, 1989) for a realist argument along these lines.
3. For this general understanding of Gandhi's teaching, see Mohandas K. Gandhi, *Gandhi: An Autobiography—The Story of My Experiments with Truth* (Boston: Beacon Press, 1957); see also Raghavan Iyer's Foreword to Puri, *Gandhi*, pp. vii–viii, n. 1.
4. George Konrad, *Anti-Politics* (New York: Harcourt Brace, 1984); Adam Michnik, *Letters from Prison* (Berkeley, CA: University of California Press, 1985); and Vaclav Havel, *Disturbing the Peace* (New York: Knopf, 1990).
5. For statements of her outlook, see Aung San Suu Kyi, *Freedom From Fear and Other Writings* (London: Penguin, 1991).
6. For a perceptive discussion along these lines, see Nikil Aziz, "The Human Rights Discourse in an Era of Globalization: Hegemony of Discourse," in *Debating Human Rights: Critical Essays from the United States and Asia*, edited by Peter Van Ness, (New York: Routledge, 2000), pp. 32–55.
7. Gandhi's decision to leave South Africa reflected his understanding that there were contexts not amenable to his methods of struggle.

Chapter 8

1. Compare Robert Pinsky's similar affirmation in "Eros Against Esperanto," in *For Love of Country*, edited by Joshua Cohen (Boston, MA: Beacon Press, 1998), pp. 85–90.

Index

Afghanistan 87–89
Algeria 45
Amnesty International 97
Annan, Kofi 24
Aquino, Benigno 149
Aquino, Corazon 86
Arab-Israeli conflict 50, 65
Arias Sánchez, Oscar 108
Aristotle 128; "golden mean" 128
Asian financial crisis 19
Ataturk, Kemal 44–46, 64
Aubrey, Edwin E. ix
Aum Shinrikyō 26
Aung San Suu Kyi 108–9
Austria 117

Baha'is 148
Bateson, Gregory 92–93
Baudridlard, Jean 101
Berrigan, Daniel 105, 142, 144
Berrigan, Philip 105, 142, 144
Bharatiya Janata Party (BJP) 48, 155–56
Birkenau camp 95–96
Bismarck, Otto von 126
Bitburg cemetery 95
Blair, Tony 58, 74
Blaisdell, Kekuni ix
Boff, Leonardo 104
Bosnia 37, 52, 117
Brazil 97, 109
Briand-Kellogg Pact (1928) 129
Browning, William 113–14
Buber, Martin ix
Buddhism 93
Bull, Hedley 15
Bush, George 95–96, 113–14

capitalism 5; market forces 53, 71, 117–18, 138; world capitalist order 81
Cassirer, Ernst 39–40
Castro, Fidel 84, 98
Charter 77 150
Chile 159
China 49–50, 75, 81, 145, 158
Christian Europe 131–34
Christianity 13, 36–37, 52–53, 55–57, 64, 83–91, 123–42
citizenship 29, 31, 116, 119; and accountability 87; "citizen pilgrim" 31, 120
civilization 9, 53–55, 81–82
Clinton, Bill 74
CNN 107, 119, 157
Cold War 52, 57, 69, 81, 85–87, 90, 98, 102, 111, 116, 126, 138, 151; Cold War Era 63
Colombia 86
Commission on Global Governance 131, 135–37
Confucianism 50
consumerism 2, 10
Copenhagen social summit 23
Cost Rica 152–53
Croatia 117
Cuba 84
Czechoslovakia 150

Dalai Lama 104, 108, 112
dangerous classes 20
dangerous knowledge 59
Democracy; "democratic peace" 27; global democracy 74

democratic peace 27
Descartes, René 42
D'Escoto, Miguel 84
Disney World 118
Douglass, James ix, 144
Doyle, Michael x

Egypt 88
El Salvador 87, 106
Enlightenment 8, 13, 15, 35, 40, 134, 139
Erasmus 128
Erbakan, Necmettin 45
Esquival Pérez, Adolpho 108
Eurocentricism 78, 128
Europe 131–32
European Union (EU) 27, 57

Foucault, Michel 103
Fox, Matthew 104
France 50–51, 93–94, 117
French Revolution 40
Fulan Gong 49–50
fundamentalism 3, 43, 67, 80, 134; Christian 89–90
futurism 82

Galileo 53
Gandhi, Mahatma 30, 48, 105–7, 112, 143–56
geopolitics 27, 119, 141; geopolitical leadership 75; new geopolitics 6
Germany 109, 117, 124, 140
Giddens, Anthony 58
global apartheid 21–22
global civil society 5–6, 41, 73, 100, 101–22, 120–21, 136
Global Compact 23
Global Democracy 74, 120, 161–62
Global Ethic Foundation 138
globalization 3, 17, 19–20, 22, 24, 50–54, 58, 61–75, 88, 123–24, 153; corporate-led 91, 137; defined 61–62; globalization from above 73, 117–18, 120, 162–63; globalization from below 29, 73–75, 120, 162–63; "humane globalization" 10, 165; and

Information Age 100; neoliberal 161
Gorbachev, Mikhail 108, 150
Great Britain 117
Green politics 97, 100
Grotius, Hugo 14, 128
Ground Zero 144
Group of Seven (G–7) 28
Gulf War (1991) 50, 110–14, 118–19, 146, 154

Hassan II (King of Morocco) 46
Havel, Vaclav 106, 150
Heaven's Gate 26
Hegel, Georg Wilhelm Friederich 14
hegemony 26
Hinduism 47–48, 51, 89, 144–45, 155–56
Hiroshima 95
Hitler, Adolph 127, 129
Hobbes, Thomas 41
Holocaust 65
human rights 7–8, 38, 54–55, 68, 107, 121
humane governance 4–6, 13–33, 58, 75, 137; "inhumane governance" 16–25
Huntington, Samuel 54, 58, 68, 123

India 47–49, 106, 109, 145, 155
InterAction Council 131, 133, 137
International Criminal Tribunal for the former Yugoslavia 37
International Monetary Fund (IMF) 3, 8, 18, 23, 73, 119, 141, 154
International Physicians for Social Responsibility 97
intifada 15, 52
Iran 45–48, 56, 64, 67, 79, 88–89, 147–49
Iraq 88, 148–49
Isaacson, Walter 127
Islam 44–45, 48, 51–52, 56, 65–66, 70, 114
Israel 65

Japan 109
Jefferson, Thomas 127
Jerusalem 65

Jesus 78, 144
John Paul II, Pope 98, 112, 131–32
John XXIII, Pope 120
Jonah House 105
Jonas, Hans 134
Judaism 65–66

Kahn, Herman 82
Kant, Immanuel 14, 41, 125
Kelly, Petra 106
Khatami, Mohammed 47, 49, 51
Khomeini, Ruhollah x, 46–47, 79, 88, 147–48
Kierkegaard, Søren ix
King, Jr., Martin Luther 106, 143–44
Kissinger, Henry 126–29
Konrad, George 150
Kosovo 7, 23, 37, 52, 117, 153–54
Küng, Hans 69, 123–42
Kyoto Protocol on Climate Change 140

Lafontaine, Oskar 140–41
League of Nations 26, 128
Lenin 43
liberalism 10, 91
Liberation theology 43, 79, 97, 114
Luther, Martin 28
Luthuli, Albert 106

Maastricht Treaty 72
Machiavelli, Niccolò 41
Mandela, Nelson 85, 159
Manicheanism 90
Maquire, Mairead 108
Marxism 28, 43, 63, 67, 80–85, 93, 145, 147
McDonalds 107
McDougal, Myres S. 5, 15
McNamara, Robert 41
Menchu, Rigoberta 108
Metternich (Chancellor) 126
Michnik, Adam 150
Mill, John Stuart 14
Milosevic, Slobodan 37
modernity 3–4, 46–47, 77–100
monarchy 45–47
Montaigne, Michel de 42

Mufti of Jerusalem 112
Muzaffar, Chandra ix
Myanmar (Burma) 108–9, 152–53

Napoleonic Wars 126
negative capability 4
Nehru, Jawaharlal 48, 106, 144–45
neoliberalism 27, 53, 57, 62, 140–41, 161
netizens 21
New Zealand 93–94
Nicaragua 84; Sandinistas 84
Nietzsche, Friedrich 63, 104
Nigeria 109
Nobel Peace Prize 97, 108–9
Non-governmental organizations (NGOs) 74
nonviolence 144–56, 160–62
non-Western 14, 38, 43–44, 48, 56–57, 68, 79, 91
North American Free Trade Agreement (NAFTA) 27
North Atlantic Treaty Organization (NATO) 7, 61
Northrop, F.S.C. ix
nuclear war 17
nuclear weapons 25
nuclearism 48, 155; nuclear weaponry 102
Nuremberg 87; Nuremberg Principles 106

Obando y Bravo, Miguel 85
Ottawa Treaty on Anti-Personnel Landmines (1997) 71, 140
Ottoman Empire 44–45, 65

Pakistan 155
Palestine 65, 151–52
Pamuk, Orhan 4
Parliament of the World's Religions 68, 133, 136, 138
Parliamentarians for Global Action 131
People Power 149–50
Peru 146
Philippines 85, 149–50
Pinochet, Augusto 37
Poland 86, 89, 150

postmodernism 36, 54, 67, 77–100, 102–103; reconstructive 11, 103, 115–22
poverty 5, 17, 19, 90, 114, 153
premodernity 77–78, 81, 84
Princeton University 163
public goods 22, 24, 28

Rainbow Warrior 93–94
Reagan, Ronald 95
realism 125–33, 140
regionalism 9, 57–58, 72–73; "compassionate region" 57
religion 13, 25–33, 62–63, 69–70, 78, 96, 104–5, 123–42; and compassion 69; exclusivist 68; inclusivist 68
religious resurgence 1–2, 16, 62–70, 91–97, 135, 164–65
Reza Shah 46
Reza Shah, Mohammed 46, 88, 147–49
Rich, Adrienne 122
Richelieu (Cardinal) 126–27
robots 2–3
Rome Treaty to Establish International Criminal Court (1998) 71, 140
Romero, Oscar (Archbishop) 114
Roosevelt, Theodore 126
Rugova, Ibrahim 153
Rumania 150
Rushdie, Salmon 51

Saddam Hussein 110–114, 118
Sanctuary Movement 87, 106
Saudi Arabia 47
Schröder, Gerhard 74
science fiction 82
secularism 16, 30, 35–52, 64, 91; "secular fundamentalism" 43
self-determination 52, 79, 116, 163
Sin, Jaime (Cardinal) 85
Smithsonian Institution 95
Snyder, Gary 93
social democracy 53, 62
socialism 20, 28, 74
Solidarity Movement 86, 150
Somalia 23
Soros, George 74

South Africa 34, 162
South Korea 85
sovereignty 37, 72
Soviet Union 32, 52, 74, 150, 159
Speer, Albert 41
Sri Lanka 89
State 2–4, 6, 19, 26, 33, 36–37, 54–55; "compassionate state" 54; "cruel state" 53; nation-state 7, 52; sovereign 116; state system 72; statism 26, 71
Strong, Maurice 23
Suarez, Francisco 128

technology 2–3, 24–25, 58–59, 158–59; Information Age 100; Information technology (IT) 61; Internet 61–62
Thailand 109
Thich Nhat Hanh 104, 112
Third Way 58
Thucydides 41
Tillich, Paul ix
Tocqueville, Alexis de 42
Toulmin, Stephen 57
Tupac Amaru 146
Turkey 44–46, 56, 64, 88
Tutu, Desmond 108, 112
Twain, Mark 158

United Nations 15–16, 22–24, 26, 33, 73, 94, 128–29; Security Council 7, 118; Security Council reform 109–10
United States 7, 20, 42, 50, 56, 73, 75, 81, 148, 158, 163; and global democracy 73; and Gulf War 111–13; role of 2

Versailles Peace Treaty 129
Vietnam War 41, 87, 142, 163
Vitoria, Francisco de 128

Walesa, Lech 86
war 61–62
West 9–10, 13, 35–36, 38, 53, 55–58, 68, 80, 82, 91–97, 158; Greek heritage 4; Westernization 49, 90, 141

Westphalia   6–8, 13, 39–40, 129
Williams, Betty   108
Wilson, Woodrow   126, 128–30
World Bank   3, 8, 18, 23, 73, 119, 154
World Economic forum (Davas)   18, 28, 74
world order   27, 35
World Order Models Project (WOMP)   15, 131, 134–36

World Trade Organization (WTO)   3, 8, 18, 23, 27–28, 73, 142

Yeats, William Butler   97
Yugoslavia   117, 121

Zapatistas   146
Zionism   65–66